GLOBAL AWAKENING

How 20th-Century Revivals Triggered a Christian Revolution

Mark Shaw

IVP Academic

An imprint of InterVarsity Press
Downers Grove, Illinois

InterVarsity Press
P.O. Box 1400, Downers Grove, IL 60515-1426
World Wide Web: www.ivpress.com
E-mail: email@ivpress.com

InterVarsity Press® is the book-publishing division of InterVarsity Christian Fellowship/USA®, a movement of
students and faculty active on campus at hundreds of universities, colleges and schools of nursing in the United States
of America, and a member movement of the International Fellowship of Evangelical Students. For information
about local and regional activities, write Public Relations Dept., InterVarsity Christian Fellowship/USA, 6400
Schroeder Rd., P.O. Box 7895, Madison, WI 53707-7895, or visit the IVCF website at <www.intervarsity.org>.

All Scripture quotations, unless otherwise indicated, are taken from the Holy Bible, New International Version®.
NIV®. Copyright ©1973, 1978, 1984 by International Bible Society. Used by permission of Zondervan Publishing
House. All rights reserved.

Design: Cindy Kiple
Images: cross collage: Gordan Poropat/iStockphoto
         Bolivian church service: Christopher Pillitz/Getty Images

ISBN 978-0-8308-3877-6

Printed in the United States of America ∞

Library of Congress Cataloging-in-Publication Data

Shaw, Mark, 1949-
  Global awakening: how 20th-century revivals triggered a Christian
revolution / Mark Shaw.
      p. cm.
  Includes bibliographical references and index.
  ISBN 978-0-8308-3877-6 (pbk.: alk. paper)
  1. Revivals—Developing countries—History—20th century. 2.
Developing countries—Church history—20th century. I. Title.
  BV3777.D44S52 2010
  269'.240917240904—dc22
                                                                      2010000183

P	20	19	18	17	16	15	14	13	12	11	10	9	8	7	6	5	4	3	2	1
Y	27	26	25	24	23	22	21	20	19	18	17	16	15	14	13	12	11	10		

To my mother, Ellen Shaw, a lover of books and a woman of faith,

With love and gratitude

CONTENTS

1

BEYOND THE SAWDUST TRAIL

The Dynamics of Global Revival

Just before dawn on April 18, 1906, America was shaken by one of the greatest natural disasters in its history. An earthquake, lasting only a minute, destroyed the city of San Francisco. By the time ensuing fires had subsided, twenty-five thousand buildings lay in ruins, a quarter million people were homeless and nearly seven hundred lives were lost. In the words of one survivor "it was bedlam, pandemonium and hell rolled into one."[1]

The San Francisco earthquake of 1906 is a grim but fitting metaphor for much of the twentieth century. It was a century of volatile political and military earthquakes and consuming ideological fires. The result was violence. Historian Niall Ferguson states that "the hundred years after 1900 was without question the bloodiest century in history."[2] There were many causes behind this violent century but Ferguson highlights one in particular: volatility. Volatile empires rose and fell. Volatile economies created uncertainty about the future. Volatile

---

[1]For the story of the San Francisco earthquake see Simon Winchester, *A Crack in the Edge of the World: America and the Great California Earthquake of 1906* (San Francisco: HarperCollins, 2006). The quotation is from "The San Francisco Earthquake, 1906," EyeWitness to History <www.eyewitnesstohistory.com> (1997).

[2]Niall Ferguson, *The War of the World: Twentieth-Century Conflict and the Descent of the West* (New York: Penguin, 2006), p. xxxiv. Ferguson documents this statement in the appendix.

encounters between ethnicities produced assimilation on the one hand and new levels of racial hatred on the other. The twentieth century was an age of earthquakes.

Yet one earthquake has passed unnoticed by Ferguson and a host of historians. It was a cultural and spiritual earthquake whose oddity in the modern world was as remarkable as it was important. I refer to the resurgence of Christianity around the world. In the face of its decline in the West, Christianity in Africa, Asia and Latin America underwent a century of dramatic growth. How high might the comeback of Christianity (and religion in general) rank compared to these other massive quakes? Philip Jenkins, author of *The Next Christendom*, thinks it might top the chart. "I suggest," writes Jenkins, "that it is precisely religious changes that are the most significant, and even the most revolutionary, in the contemporary world."[3]

Many experts were surprised by this development. Growing secularization in the world was supposed to plunge religion in general and Christianity in particular into permanent decline. Just the opposite happened. How could a doomed faith overcome the powers of secularization and become such a force of revolutionary cultural change? One must think globally to answer this question. When one looks beyond Atlantic shores the most significant change in the world in the last several generations is the broader revival of religion sweeping the southern hemisphere. To miss this global development, writes Jenkins, would be "on par with a review of the eighteenth century that managed to miss the French revolution."[4]

Missing the French Revolution would be bad enough but other analogies come to mind. If, like me, you have watched with concern the sharp decline of Western Christianity since the 1960s something more is at stake. To miss the rise and significance of the new World Christianity would be like a concerned Christian in sixteenth-century north-

---

[3]Philip Jenkins, *The Next Christendom: The Coming of Global Christianity* (New York: Oxford University Press, 2002), p. 1.
[4]Ibid.

ern Europe missing Luther and the Reformation. Something that affects the renewal of Christianity worldwide is afoot and no one should miss the party.

The fact of Christianity's global comeback is undeniable. Africa went from ten million Christians in 1900 to four hundred million in 2000. Pentecostalism went from a handful in 1906 to half a billion worldwide by century's end.[5] The center of Christianity shifted from North America and Europe to Africa, Asia and Latin America. Jenkins calls this shift "one of the transforming moments in the history of religion worldwide."[6] One can sense the epic nature of these shifts, but how deeply do we understand the causes and implications of this earthquake? What do the statistics mean?[7]

Experts on World Christianity explain these statistics by pointing to a wide variety of powerful factors. There were missionaries everywhere. Evangelicals called for conversion. National Christians eagerly shared the good news in word and deed. Bibles were translated into vernacular languages. Christianity became indigenized into new people groups. It became inculturated into new worldviews. It discovered contextualization and fought injustices around the world. Globalization had a role to play. New nation-states failed to deliver and sent locals scurrying for spiritual alternatives. Pentecostalism seemed to speak everybody's language. And then there was God, at work behind the scenes orchestrating this great symphony of religious revolution.[8]

I do not deny these expert answers. I agree with all of them, in fact.

---

[5]For the most extensive published statistics on World Christianity see David B. Barrett, George Thomas Kurian and Todd M. Johnson, *World Christian Encyclopedia: A Comparative Survey of Churches and Religions in the Modern World A.D. 30–A.D. 2200,* 2nd ed. (New York: Oxford University Press, 2001).

[6]Jenkins, *Next Christendom,* pp. 1-2.

[7]For a competent and insightful survey of the shift of Christianity see Dana L. Robert, "Shifting Southward: Global Christianity Since 1945," *International Bulletin of Missionary Research* 24, no. 2 (2000).

[8]For an informed summary of the main factors contributing to the rise of twentieth-century World Christianity see Brian Stanley, "Twentieth-Century World Christianity: A Perspective from the History of Missions," in *Chrisianity Reborn: The Global Expansion of Evangelicalism in the Twentieth Century,* ed. Donald M. Lewis (Grand Rapids: Eerdmans, 2004).

Christian resurgence is a complex matter involving a complex of causes. One factor, however, has been underemphasized in the telling of the tale. It is a factor that in many ways acted as a delivery system for many of the other forces just mentioned. I am referring to revival.

Revivals? Aren't revivals quirky folk rituals associated with rural America and nineteenth-century camp meetings? Didn't they pass out of fashion with hula hoops and Edsels? For many, revivals are little more than relics of a distant past. They belong more to an age of plows and prairies than of postmodernity and globalization. And like King Arthur's sword in the stone, the term may be so deeply embedded in American folk culture that any attempt to extract it is doomed to failure.

Yet the sword in the stone is moving. The news of revivalism's death has been greatly exaggerated. Revivals, like forces of nature, are protean, constantly adjusting their features and ferocity to new times and to new places. In the twentieth century these American "folk rituals" packed up their tents and sawdust trails and went global. They learned to speak Spanish, Portuguese, Yoruba, Korean, Mandarin and Gujarati. They crossed the equator. As they traveled abroad they grabbed hold of missionaries, Bible translations, national evangelists, globalization and glossolalia and turned them into a religious revolution. Global revivals, I want to contend in this book, are at the heart of the global resurgence of Christianity.

To persuade discerning readers that this is so requires some explanation and some examples. Much of the rest of this book will deal with the examples. This chapter focuses on the explanation. What are global revivals and how do they work? My search for an answer to this question began near the shores of Cape Cod during a New England boyhood.

THE DYNAMICS OF GLOBAL REVIVAL

I grew up with revivals. One doesn't normally think of the greater Boston area or its south shore as the Bible belt. Our little church, however, snuggled into a quiet corner of southeastern Massachusetts, defied the general trend. When my father was in his mid thirties he experienced a profound conversion and started attending a little Baptist church in our leafy New England village. My mother, my two sisters and I soon followed.

Our town had large numbers of Catholics, Unitarians, Methodists, Congregationalists, Episcopalians and one modest Baptist church. The pastor was a kindly fundamentalist open to the new changes that Billy Graham and other neo-evangelicals were bringing about in fundamentalist circles in the 1950s and 1960s but he also had one foot in the old-time religion. Every year our church would have revival meetings. I remember as a boy of eleven hearing Bob Jones Sr., he of Bob Jones University notoriety. He even came to dinner once. His camp meeting style still rings in my ears. But these revival meetings were little more than ritual reenactments of mighty movements that had once swept the prairies, shaken our cities and reshaped the landscape of American religion.

How did such mighty movements become so small and insignificant? Are revivals part of normative Christianity or simply an American aberration? How do they work and do they have a future? Do they happen in other parts of the world or just in America?

I pursued these questions later in seminary and found a number of answers. Two decades of studying and teaching African Christianity in Kenya added yet more light on the matter. It also convinced me that revivals were indeed global in scope and not merely tied to American history. Finally, a year at the University of Edinburgh and its Centre for the Study of World Christianity answered questions about the various dynamics that make up global revival. I confirmed the fact that revivals, while dismissed as obsolete by many, are very much alive all around the world. I now know a little more about revivals than I did when Bob Jones came to town. Here's what I've found out so far.

I begin with the pioneers. Two pathfinders in the study of global Christian revivals are J. Edwin Orr and Richard Lovelace. J. Edwin Orr in a series of global narratives chronicled the large number of nineteenth- and twentieth-century awakenings that occurred in virtually every continent.[9] Orr's understanding of the nature of these diverse revivals was quite elemental. A repetition of the phenomena of Acts 2 (mainly Spirit-inspired corporate prayer and evangelical proclamation) were the essential visible causes of revival and awakening. Though Orr's revival case studies were far ranging, his analysis of the phenomena seemed incomplete.

Richard Lovelace's contribution stood in contrast to Orr. Lovelace wrote little about global revivals but worked hard to form a new model of revival that lifted them out of an American cultural setting and freed them to be understood in a more universal way. For Lovelace, Orr's concept of revival was as theologically minimal as it was geographically expansive. More was going on in a revival than simply prayer and preaching, however central those activities might be. Lovelace sought to open up the modern understanding of revival by expanding the theological and historical model of revival beyond earlier categories.

Deeply influenced by Jonathan Edwards and his theology of revival, Lovelace improved on Orr by identifying eleven elements of spiritual renewal at the heart of evangelical revivals. This model took the study of revival to deeper levels theologically and historically.[10] Lovelace distinguished between the terms *revival, reformation* and *renewal.* Revivals "trace back to biblical metaphors for the infusion of spiritual life in Christian experience by the Holy Spirit."[11] Revivals were "broad-scale movements of the Holy Spirit's work in renewing spiritual vitality in the church and in fostering its expansion in mission and evangelism."[12] Reformation focused on "the purifying of doctrine and structures in the church, but implies also a component of spiritual revitalization."[13]

Renewal was his most comprehensive term to cover both revival and

---

[9]Cf. J. Edwin Orr, *The Flaming Tongue: The Impact of Twentieth Century Revivals* (Chicago: Moody Press, 1973).

[10]Richard Lovelace, *Dynamics of Spiritual Life* (Downers Grove, Ill.: InterVarsity Press, 1979). For his eleven elements see his chart on p. 93.

[11]Ibid., p. 21.

[12]Ibid., p. 22.

[13]Ibid.

reformation. It also denoted *"aggiornamento,* the updating of the church leading to new engagement with the surrounding world."[14] These distinctions, however valid, have not affected the common usage of the term *revival,* which still encompasses all of the above usages. Lovelace's importance lies in opening up the concept of revival to the wider implications of reform and renewal. Revivals understood in the fullest sense must incorporate spiritual, structural and social transformation.[15]

Over the years I've thought a lot about Lovelace's approach to awakenings and revival. I think, as he does, that spiritual dynamics are the most important ones in understanding revival. I agree with him that reform and social action are part of Christian revival movements. Enlarging the list of spiritual dynamics like this enriches our understanding. At the same time I think more needs to be said about different *kinds* of dynamics. A host of missiologists, anthropologists and historians have studied religious revivals of various kinds and have added to our overall understanding of such movements. Spiritual dynamics, no matter how many are mentioned, constitute just one kind of factor. Because revivals take place in history there are also historical dynamics that shape revival movements. And because revivals interact with local cultures there are also key cultural dynamics. If we accept these statements, then we may recognize that at least five different kinds of dynamics drive the charismatic people movements we call revivals. (See figure 1.)

SPIRITUAL DYNAMICS

Most definitions of revival begin, quite rightly, from a theological perspective. A typical definition describes a revival as "the work of the Holy Spirit in restoring the people of God to a more vital spiritual life, witness and work by prayer and the Word after repentance in crisis for their spiritual decline."[16] This is a good place to begin. I hear in this

---

[14]Ibid.
[15]Ibid.
[16]"Revival" in *Evangelical Dictionary of World Missions,* ed. A. Scott Moreau (Grand Rapids: Baker, 2000).

Global revivals are charismatic people movements that transform their world by translating Christian truth and transferring power.

Spiritual dynamics (Content factor—What makes a revival Christian?)
- Personal liberation—shift from rejected orphans to much-loved children
- Eschatological vision—shift from fatalism to radical hope
- Radical community—shift from alienated victims to charismatic family
- Evangelical activism—shift from survival mode to transforming mission
- Life in the Spirit—"Divine and supernatural light" who produces the four shifts and orchestrates all dynamics
- Negative Spiritual dynamics—new light extremism, old light reaction, spiritual warfare, generational conflict

Cultural dynamics (Local factor—What are the essential elements that make up a local revival?)
- People factor (indigenization): transfer of power to new leadership
- Faith factor (inculturation): translation of Christian truth into worldview
- Justice factor (contextualization): transformation of status, structures or systems

Historical dynamics (Time factor—How do revivals develop over time?)
- Problem stage: volatility that destabilizes systems
- Paradigm stage: new light, new leaders, new movements
- Power stage: conflict and conquest

Global dynamics (International factor—How do global trends influence local revivals?
- Globalization—Winds from the West: Global shrinkage and sameness
- Relativization—Crisis of the local: will we survive the West?
- Localization—The reassertion of the value of the local
- Glocalization—Revival, resurgence and global expansion of the local

Group dynamics (Variety factor—Why are Christian revivals so different in content and character?)
- Lucan variable: reviving the evangelical impulse
- Galatian variable: returning to the old ways
- Corinthian variable: radical break with past
- Group conflict: the fight for supremacy

Figure 1. Dynamics of global revivals

summary important spiritual dynamics: the Spirit's primary role, spiritual crisis, restoration and repentance, revitalized Christian community and renewed witness and work.

Though the above definition grew out of American revivalism, these themes reoccur in similar movements around the world. For this reason global revivals must be seen as more than just "people movements." They must be seen as "charismatic people movements," movements in which people testify that they were transformed by the power of God. In global revivals of an evangelical nature one commonly sees four features of a kind of classic Christianity. Each of these features is an expression of *life in the Spirit*, so central in the book of Acts (e.g., Acts 2 and 4) and in the theology of the apostles (e.g., Paul in Romans 8 and Ephesians 3).[17] They represent four shifts that move the individual and the movement out of the "world" (systems of fallen society) into the "kingdom" (the reality of the risen and ruling Christ).

The first shift is *personal liberation* where both leaders and followers testify to freedom from spiritual bondage. We move from being an unloved orphan rejected by a wrathful God to an assurance of adoption by an all-loving father. Whether one uses the propositional language of justification by faith or the metaphorical language of the prodigal son, the reality of grace, sonship and union with God through Christ fills the consciousness of the spiritually awakened.

A second spiritual dynamic is *eschatological vision*. Members of the new movement experience a shift in values and behavior from self-reliance (we can do anything) and fatalism (we can do nothing) to a bold vision of God bringing his kingdom to earth in fullness. In movements of revival, members testify to a shift in their sense of purpose and history from some achievable human vision of the future (e.g., humanist, tribal, Marxist, utopian) to a new vision of history centered upon the person and promises of Christ. He is seen as the one who controls the

---

[17]For an excellent summary of the Pauline model of life in the Spirit cf. Gordon Fee, *Paul, the Spirit and the People of God* (London: Hodder & Stoughton, 1997).

flow of history toward his intended purpose of perfectly establishing the kingdom of God.

A third dynamic is *radical community*. Alienated victims shift into charismatic family members who live lives of a glad dependence both on the risen Christ as well as on each other. This double dependence is a conscious and comprehensive dependence on Christ first and others second. Radical dependence on Christ is shown by dependent prayer and attentiveness to his word in the Bible. A new secondary dependence on the body of Christ results through whom Christ typically acts to meet needs in answer to prayer.

A fourth and final dynamic is *evangelical activism*. This represents a shift from survival mode to transforming mission. The new community turns its attention from internal growth to outward mission. This renewed mission seeks to overcome the fragmented witness of a previous time and attempts a fuller witness that involves both evangelism and social action. This holistic mission happens both locally and globally.

This classic Christianity just described defines the "new light" that inspires revived Christian movements throughout history. I will refer to revival leaders and followers who profess and proclaim aspects of this four dimensional life in the Spirit as "new lights," a term borrowed from the Great Awakening of 1740 and originally applied to those whose views of renewal constituted the evangelical mainstream represented by George Whitefield, John Wesley and Jonathan Edwards. When applied to leaders of a global revival it refers to the moderate mainstream. "Old lights" are those who tend to oppose new lights. New light extremists are those who reject both old lights and moderate new lights.

Given the positive description of the spiritual dynamics of global revivals one might be tempted to view such movements as unmixed blessings to church and society. Biblical realism should prevent such a hasty conclusion, however. J. I. Packer has warned of the "romantic fallacy" about revivals. For some, awakenings are Edenlike experiences of

Christian unity, vitality and potency.[18] The reality is often quite different. There is vitality. There are often new expressions of unity. There is undoubtedly a great deal of spiritual potency. Yet in both the Bible and in history, revivals are also times of intense conflict, opposition and tension. Negative spiritual dynamics operate alongside positive ones. Negative dynamics include new light extremism that moves beyond Scripture, old light reaction that rejects the revival as satanic or insane, spiritual warfare with supernatural evil as well as the inevitable generation gap in which older people tend not to get it and younger new lights are eventually displaced by a generation that is ignorant of the powerful work of God in their parents' time. Despite the presence of negative spiritual dynamics, positive spiritual dynamics linked to life in the Spirit abound even more.

Jonathan Edwards (1703-1758) contributed more than most to the understanding of the spiritual dynamics of revival. For Lovelace the theological insights into the inner workings of revival provided by Edwards constitute the "foundational theology of spiritual renewal in English, and perhaps in any language."[19]

Edwards' central insight is "the divine and supernatural light" that makes gospel realities real and beautiful to the believer. The Holy Spirit, for Edwards, is the source of all other dynamics of renewed spiritual life. One of the realities made vivid by the Spirit was liberation in Christ. This liberation involved both descent and ascent. "The illumination of the heart," writes Lovelace,

> which brought converts in touch with the reality of God simultaneously revealed to them how deeply sin gripped their own lives. They suddenly became aware that their problem was not isolated acts of conscious disobedience to God, but a deep aversion to God at the root of their personalities, an aversion which left them in unconscious bondage to unbelief, selfishness, jealousy and other underlying complexes of sin.

---

[18]J. I. Packer, *A Quest for Godliness: The Puritan Vision of the Christian Life* (Wheaton, Ill.: Crossway, 1990), p. 317.
[19]Lovelace, *Dynamics of Spiritual Life*, pp. 38-39.

What was so great about the awakening was not this stressful consciousness of sin but the profound relief of this stress through a new vision of Jesus Christ who offered through his cross "the only righteousness that could reconcile such depravity to a holy God."[20]

From this personal liberation flowed a postmillennial vision of history in which an exalted Christ returns to an earth transformed by a revived global church. This revived church experienced radical love for God and one another and practiced dependent prayer. Revived souls and communities moved from narrow concepts of service and mission to more holistic evangelism and social action. Edwards envisioned a new mission to the Stockbridge Indians of western Massachusetts as presaging a new era in crosscultural missions around the world. The mission would not simply be in word only but also in practical love, the most reliable and final of the twelve signs of true spirituality mentioned in Edwards' *Religious Affections*.

Edwards, however, was realistic about revivals no matter how much he seemed smitten by their spiritual beauty. In each of his major studies he documented the carnality, extremism and excesses that are the bane of revivals and awakenings in every era and every culture. Yet the revival bottom line for Edwards was a positive one. The assets of revival outweighed their liabilities and should be encouraged by church leaders everywhere.[21]

CULTURAL DYNAMICS

Global revivals are spiritual movements shaped by spiritual dynamics. But that is not all they are. Because revivals take place in a particular

---

[20]Ibid.

[21]Edwards wrote four major works on revival, many of which have remained in print for over two hundred years: *A Faithful Narrative of Surprising Conversions* (1737) (with an estimated sixty editions, several of those in the last hundred years); *Distinguishing Marks of a Work of the Spirit of God* (1741); *Some Thoughts Concerning the Revival* (1743) and his culminating study, *A Treatise Concerning Religious Affections* (1746). For critical editions of these works see C. C. Goen, ed., *The Great Awakening*, The Works of Jonathan Edwards, vol. 4 (New Haven, Conn.: Yale University Press, 1972); John E. Smith, ed., *The Religious Affections*, The Works of Jonathan Edwards, vol. 2 (New Haven, Conn.: Yale University Press, 1959).

context, an additional set of dynamics come into play. Missiologists toss out terms like *indigenization, inculturation* and *contextualization* with confusing regularity. But don't let the clumsiness of these terms conceal the deeper truth. Though missiologists frequently speak as though these three terms are synonyms, I would contend that each term has something unique to contribute. These dynamics are powerful and distinct forces behind global revivals. Let's take a closer look at these three factors.

The people factor. The first cultural dynamic is indigenization. At the heart of this force is the transfer of power from vested interests to a new people, often previously marginalized. Global revivals most often involve indigenous people. Local people become led by local leaders, often prophetic figures proclaiming a "new light" that leads people forward into the future. In indigenization power and leadership pass from a missionary generation or an older generation to locals or the young. In global revivals new leaders often come not from the ranks of the rich and the powerful but from below. Leaders and followers from marginalized groups (e.g., women, youth, the poor) receive a new map of reality and begin to move forward together down those new roads.

Evan Roberts (1878-1951) was one of fourteen children born to coal miner Henry Roberts and his wife Hannah. Though he became a blacksmith's apprentice, his real passion was Christian ministry even though the glories of the Welsh Calvinist Methodist Church were long past. By the time Roberts was twenty-five he had the kind of spiritual encounter that would characterize new light leaders in Africa, Asia and Latin America in the rest of the century.

In 1904 Roberts experienced an "anointing" by the Holy Spirit. He started holding prayer meetings at his home. These meetings were full of remarkable spontaneity with young people singing, confessing and testifying with a fervor that sometimes went on all night. This youth revival soon spilled over into the wider church. By the time the revival fires waned some one hundred thousand converts had joined the movement, and many times that number were influenced by its teaching and

21

spirituality. The movement was an indigenous revival, led by young people with few formal credentials. Though it eventually cut across the class structure of Wales and the United Kingdom it began with marginalized segments of the population. The Welsh revival was to have a worldwide influence on many subsequent global revivals, and the power of indigenization would be at the forefront.

The faith factor. Revivals have more than leaders. They also have a heart. Along with the people factor is the faith factor. Revivals help trigger a process missiologists call *inculturation* which takes place when the gospel is heard on the deep worldview level of the hearer. It connects with concerns and convictions deeply held.

Andrew Walls, noted historian of World Christianity, describes it as a translation process. The process has two dimensions. One is the *indigenous* or *homing principle* whereby a people hear God speak their language and sense his gracious presence in their lives and culture. He accepts them as they are as Africans, Asians, Latinos, Arabs or Anglos. The realities of classic Christianity—God as father, Christ as Lord, the Spirit as God's empowering presence, apostolic community and mission—all explode into bold relief in the depths of one's mind and heart taking over the worldview.

This explosion of divine acceptance and presence produces a surprising second aspect of the translation process. Walls calls this the *pilgrim principle.* The new people of God now see themselves defined by more than their particular ethnicity and history. They see themselves as part of a larger story and a larger world, a story that begins with Israel and moves to the nations. Inculturation thus produces a psychic explosion that roots the gospel in the depths of one's being.[22]

In 1905, Pandita Ramabai (1858-1922), Indian Christian leader and founder of the Mukti ("salvation") mission for destitute girls near Pune, India, saw an evangelical revival break out among her students. Her own dramatic conversion to Christianity in 1891 out of high-caste

---

[22]Andrew F. Walls, *The Missionary Movement in Christian History: Studies in the Transmission of Faith* (Maryknoll, N.Y.: Orbis, 1996).

Hinduism prepared her for what followed. Though the revival eventually witnessed a similar outbreak of tongues as was seen in the Azusa revival of the following year, the heart of the movement was a new vision of God, personal liberation, eschatological vision, radical community and evangelical activism. Pandita embraced the new movement from America.

For years she had been interested in the phenomenon of revival, once sending her daughter to Australia largely to report on news that a revival was underway there. Pandita's interest in revival was not in the manifestation of tongues but in the new vision of Christ and his excellencies at the heart of an evangelical revival. She also longed for renewal of her Christian community at Mukti and new energy in its mission. Her own experience of conversion as an intense spiritual enlightenment instilled within her the conviction that the revivals would bring refreshment and energy on all these levels. She encouraged her Bible women to de-emphasize glossolalia and emphasize the content of the gospel as they preached in the nearby villages and spread the revival throughout western India. The faith factor lies at the heart of global revival.[23] We will see this dynamic at work repeatedly in the chapters that follow.

The justice factor. Global revivals seek to change their world. Flowing out of indigenization and inculturation is a third cultural dynamic, contextualization. This is the justice factor. Revivals are both caused by change and are catalysts of change. They arise from a widespread sense of fear and uncertainty about the future. We would do well to borrow Ferguson's concept of volatility. Revivals are not generally caused by stagnation in the church. Something more dramatic is needed. The soil into which the seed of revival is sown is one of discontent, uncertainty and volatility. The twentieth century's fluctuations within capitalism, colonialism and world war affected so many local contexts that volatility and fear were in large supply. Under the guidance of their new light

---

[23]Edith Blumhofer, "Consuming Fire: Pandita Ramabai and the Global Pentecostal Impulse" (Institute for the Study of American Evangelicals, 2001).

leaders people saw the way forward, the way to redefine their reality and behave as liberated people rather than colonized masses or impoverished citizens. They build new churches, new schools, new agencies, new political parties and act with an independence of spirit that makes it clear that their status has been changed in key ways and that they expect the system to change as a result.

In 1906 the Azusa Street revival began in Los Angeles under the leadership of African American evangelist William Seymour. Seymour proclaimed that the end was near and that God was baptizing his people with tongues of the Spirit in order to raise up a mighty missionary force that would reach the world prior to the return of Christ. One of the remarkable features of the revival was its interracial character. Los Angeles was notorious for its racial tensions. Yet here in the heart of this cauldron of prejudice was a movement of racial reconciliation that was startling in its force and scope. Decades before the civil rights movement of the 1960s, white and black worshiped, wept and went to the ends of the earth together, all inspired by a black revivalist.

Though racism would rear its head in later American Pentecostalism, this early and unexpected expression of racial harmony was a reminder of the social power of revivals. They are movements of contextualization, movements that seek to change their world in startling and significant ways. Azusa Street, perhaps even more than the Welsh revival, would help stimulate thousands of similar movements in Africa, Asia and Latin America. These new movements would become forces of justice from below. Racial, tribal and ethnic boundaries would be broken. New expressions of human reconciliation would be unleashed. With few exceptions, global revivals are movements of justice.

HISTORICAL DYNAMICS

Global revivals are not only movements of the Spirit that interact with culture and context. They are also movements of history. Describing the spiritual and cultural dynamics behind global revivals still leaves unanswered the question of what these movements look like in real life.

24

Global movements don't just appear out of thin air. Revivals move through time and space.

In 1956, American anthropologist, Anthony Wallace, after studying hundreds of "revitalization" movements, suggested a typical historical pattern. We can simplify his model by talking about three critical stages in movements of revitalization and revival. Global revivals are conceived during the problem stage, explode on the scene during the paradigm stage and begin to change their world as they mature during a final power stage.[24] (See figure 2.)

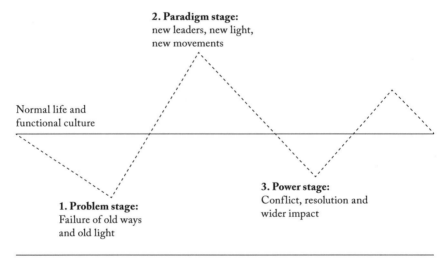

2. **Paradigm stage:**
new leaders, new light,
new movements

Normal life and
functional culture

3. **Power stage:**
Conflict, resolution and
wider impact

1. **Problem stage:**
Failure of old ways
and old light

Figure 2. Typical historical pattern of global revivals

The problem stage. Prior to the outbreak of a revival, people in a given context feel that their maps of reality no longer work. The old ways appear to be dead ends. It could be because of globalizing forces such as a colonial takeover, war, an economic roller coaster or an internal crisis destroys confidence in the shared worldview. Often a new dominant culture creates a crisis of confidence in a minority culture.

At first a few young people may register the death of the old ways by

---

[24]The original essay appears in Anthony Wallace, *Revitalization and Mazeways: Essays on Culture Change,* ed. Robert S. Grument, vol. 1 (Lincoln: University of Nebraska Press, 2003).

bizarre, antisocial behavior. After these isolated cases wider social dislocation occurs. Alcoholism, marital breakdown, and other signs of severe cultural stress become widespread. Old light conservatives diagnose the problem as a departure from tradition. Radicals emerge calling for a complete abandonment of the old ways and radical new solutions to the social and cultural malaise. There is a desperate need for a new paradigm, a new map of reality that will help people get unstuck.

For Christian groups this means that their theological and spirituality systems seem to fail. Theological conservatives advise stricter adherence to the creeds or rituals. Theological radicals call for starting over from square one or adopting the views of the dominant culture.

The paradigm stage. From the masses a leader or group of leaders emerge who are neither reactionaries nor radicals. These new light moderates often come out of an experience of brokenness during stage one. In the midst of their despair God speaks in a new way. He calls them back to the New Testament. He shows them the beauty of new covenant realities. He renews his promises and commands. They undergo a dramatic conversion or recommitment. Like the rod of Moses the power of classic Christianity parts the waters. A new way forward appears. The leader proclaims the new paradigm to others. Disciples respond and increase, testifying to a conversion experience similar to the leader. The numbers grow. Soon one prophet's vision becomes a mass movement. New structures are built to support the movement. A revival is born.

The power stage. As the movement grows reactionaries and radicals attack the new movement. Resistance from the surrounding culture increases. If the movement is able to resolve the conflict with conservatives and radicals, then its influence grows, and it begins to make changes in the spiritual system that often have implications for the social, political and economic systems. Social capital is built. The new convert becomes employable. They take seriously their family role. New acts of service bring healing to broken institutions and families within the culture. Cultural renewal takes place. Mission efforts expand the movement even beyond local or regional borders. The new movement may become crosscultural and international if successful.

This multistage process appears throughout both biblical and post biblical history. The fact of decline/volatility (problem stage) and renewal (new paradigm and new power) is connected to covenant renewal in both Testaments. Beginning with the covenant with Abraham and later the generation of Moses, much Old Testament history is the story of covenant breaking and the enormous spiritual, social, political and economic fallout that results. New voices arise, a Daniel, an Isaiah, a Hannah, to call the people back to the covenant in repentance and renewal. New surges of spiritual and national vitality often accompany these movements of covenant renewal in Israel's history. This pattern continues in the New Testament when the new covenant is proclaimed by Jesus of Nazareth and initiated by his death and resurrection.

The Jesus movement breaks out in Acts 2 hungry for mission and determined to turn the world upside down. Yet after sweet seasons of spiritual vitality, the people of God run out of steam (as seen in Galatians, Hebrews and the letters to the churches in Revelation). Renewal is needed. New leaders emerge and drink deeply from new covenant sources. Their eyes are opened, and they translate the gospel for new times. New highways appear in the desert.

Christian historians such as Kenneth Scott Latourette and Andrew Walls document how this broad tidal pattern of spiritual decline and revitalization has continued down through the centuries following the close of the first century. Revivals are smaller instances of this larger pattern of decline and renewal, streams that feed this larger river. Thus times of perceived decline create the longing for change. Revivals restore the spiritual dynamics of Christianity and lead to new movements or renewed institutions. The wider consequences of revival produce the fruits of change (in small or large ways) in one's world.

GLOBAL AND GROUP DYNAMICS

Two other kinds of dynamics are at play in global revivals. The larger one is external and global, and the smaller one is internal and confined to the group. I want to argue that in a world of *globalization* (where Western economic and religio-cultural forces are destabilizing traditional societies) two reactions typically occur. There is an initial stage of *relativization* in which the local traditions take a huge hit from the impact of global trends. But following this initial hit there is often a hit back through *localization*. New leaders arise to reassert the value of the local. Often vernacular Bible translations were a critical piece of this localization process. Fresh on the heels of localization may come what some sociologists call *glocalization*. Local forces kick in and begin to produce revival, resurgence and expansion. Glocalization is the local going global. The local movement, full of confidence and a sense of divine call, gets on the global highway and heads west.

The final set of dynamics is group dynamics. Throughout the case studies in this book we will see how different Christian revivals can be from one another even though they may all fall broadly under the definition I have offered above. Revivals differ often because of a movement's attitudes about tradition. In the Lucan variable a revival movement seeks to transcend tradition by going back to the golden age of the apostles and drinking deeply from those original sources. In the Galatian type a movement works overtime to preserve tradition, often fairly recent tradition. In the Corinthian variable a revival seizes the opportunity to break from the past and start over. I will mention more about these group dynamics and their importance in the final chapter.

What do we end up with if we combine these five different dynamics of a global revival together into a single definition? *Global revivals* are *charismatic people movements that seek to transform their world by translating Christian truth and transferring power.* Global forces often set the stage for these movements. The message of the kingdom is proclaimed by a missionary or native evangelist in the context of globalizing forces little understood by the locals. New light leaders trigger the *people factor* (rise of indigenous leaders and followers representing the transfer of spiritual authority and power), the *faith factor* (the translation of classic Christian truth into new contexts) and *the justice factor* (contextualization as transformation of one's world). Through the power of the Holy Spirit, revivals bring to marginalized people spiritual liberation, a new vision of history, radical community and evangelical activism (classic Christianity). They also bring power struggles, extremism and shattered unity.

As historical movements, revivals begin with problems. Their soil is often that of social volatility and the failure of older forms of the faith or traditional religion to deal with that volatility. Out of the ashes of the old springs the new. New leaders emerge and form a movement that ends up clashing with the established powers. If the movement can resolve those clashes, it then moves outward to alter the social, spiritual and cultural landscape of the surrounding world.

THE ROAD AHEAD

I've made some large claims in the last few pages. Beyond my description of the various dynamics that create revival movements, I've claimed something more. Revivals lie behind much of the diversity and size of the new World Christianity. I am not claiming that they are the only factor in Christian resurgence. The religious revolution of the twentieth century can't be explained by any one factor. I am, however, claiming that global revivals act as the delivery system for a variety of forces and factors that account for global Christian growth, vitality and diversity.

The religious revolution of the twentieth century didn't begin with high profile events like the World Parliament of Religion in the 1890s or the famous Edinburgh mission conference of 1910. These movements were important in the development of inter-religious dialogue and the emergence of the ecumenical movement respectively. But they shed little light on the biggest religious development of the century—the rise of a new World Christianity. Looking back over the last ten decades the real story of World Christianity starts not from above but from below, with indigenous movements of translated Christianity. The story of World Christianity is a story of a great and global awakening.

The story goes something like this. The Welsh revival of 1904 was the first tremor of the larger quake to come. Its aftershock saw larger shudders of renewal in Azusa Street, India and Korea. The Azusa Street revival, as mentioned above, sent its witnesses throughout the Americas, Africa, Europe and Asia in the decade after 1906. Africa experienced several waves of revival during the century. In southern Africa the violent eschatology of the Watchtower Society triggered a cluster of apocalyptic revival movements in South Africa, the Rhodesias (now Zimbabwe and Zambia) and as far north as Congo. The rise of important prophet figures like William Wade Harris, Simon Kimbangu and Joseph Babalola in the first thirty years of the twentieth century saw new churches formed out of powerful movements of the Spirit. The East African revival of the 1930s and 1940s stayed largely in the mission churches but brought an evangelical depth and charismatic openness that breathed new life into aging structures. These earlier waves of revival paved the way for the largest cluster of revivals, those associated with the neo-Pentecostal churches that have arisen and proliferated since the mid-1970s.

The Latin American scene bears strong similarities to the African story. Azusa Street missionaries found their way to Chile, Mexico and Brazil by 1910. Brazil, as the largest nation in Latin America, reflects a story found generally across the Latin American landscape. Several waves of revival in the 1910s, 1950s and 1980s produced massive church growth largely of evangelical and Pentecostal varieties. The fastest growing segment of Roman Catholicism in Brazil, the largest Catholic country in the world, was among Catholic charismatics.

Asia has also experienced numerous revival movements. The Indonesian revival of 1965 saw several million Muslims and traditionalists move en masse into Christian churches. The Korean revival of 1907 is regarded by many Korean church historians as the key to understanding the dynamic story of Korean Christianity throughout the century. The Shantung revival of the 1930s brought into existence many of the major house church networks that have enjoyed exponential growth after the Chinese Cultural Revolution of the 1960s and 1970s. Revivals under Pandita Ramabai, V. S. Azariah and Bakt Singh are a key part of the story of the growth of the Indian church. Revivals in Southeast Asia, the Philippines and Oceania tell a similar story. Global revivals were at the heart of World Christian resurgence.

But I am getting ahead of myself. In this book I offer case studies of global revivals that show how they work and how they broker other growth factors such as indigenization, globalization and nationalism. Armed with a few basic definitions and dynamics of global revivals we are now ready to embark on a closer look at specific global movements. Let me briefly sketch out the route we will take in our global travels. In the chapters that follow we want to explore

- the Korean revival of 1907 and the role of *globalization* in creating the conditions for the rise of the new World Christianity

- the 1930 Babalola revival in Nigeria and the centrality of *indigenous leadership and the transfer of power* in the new World Christianity

- the Dornakal revival in India under V. S. Azariah and the power of *conversion* as a distinguishing mark of the new World Christianity

- the East Africa revival of the 1940s and the importance of *radical community* in producing a movement with an enduring impact

- the North American post-war evangelical revival and the key role of *international networking* in globalizing local revival movements

- Latin American Pentecostal revivalism in Brazil since the 1970s and *the justice factor* in the new World Christianity

- neo-Pentecostal revivalism in Ghana in the 1980s and 1990s and the importance of *eschatological vision and global mission* in World Christianity

- the Chinese house church movement as a global revival and the role of *conflict resolution* as a critical factor in changing their world

In the final chapter I'll try to draw some lessons from these case

31

studies for those seeking to be agents of renewal in their own settings. At that point I'll also look at why global Christian revivals vary dramatically in content and character.

I visited San Francisco not long ago and like most visitors was impressed with its beauty and vitality. I watched the Giants play baseball at what was then Pac Bell Park (now AT&T Park). I feasted on the paintings of Marc Chagall at the Museum of Modern Art. I ate seafood on Fisherman's Wharf. The city had obviously recovered in spectacular style from the devastation of 1906. Yet the impact of that earthquake remains. It has redefined both the shape and skyline of San Francisco's modern form.

Similarly, twentieth-century global revivals have produced an altered religious landscape. That altered landscape created by these explosive revivals requires investigation. Seeing is believing. We need to visit the scene of the action. We need to sift though the ruins of the recent past to reconstruct these mighty movements. Our sifting begins on the other side of the Pacific in Japanese-occupied Korea.

2

ABOVE THE 38th PARALLEL

Kil Sun Ju and the
Korean Revival of 1907

Dr. Caleb Chul-Soo Kim and his wife Manok came from South Korea to Kenya as missionaries among unreached groups in East Africa. They mastered Swahili. They learned the culture. They deeply loved Africans. They were expertly prepared. Caleb had a doctorate from a U.S. graduate school. After they joined the faculty of our school, I was impressed with all that they brought to the table. I learned much about Africa through conversations with them both. I also began to learn about the church in South Korea. I became increasingly intrigued at what might lie at the root of this dynamic expression of Christianity.

Caleb grew up in the 1960s in a divided Korea suffering from right-wing dictators and constant fear of invasion from their communist neighbor to the north. In 1981 as a young twenty-one-year-old Buddhist in the army, Caleb heard the gospel for the first time by reading a Korean Bible. A personal encounter with Christ followed his reading of the Gospels and Romans. He found his way to a Presbyterian church where he eventually met and married Manok, whose family had been Christians for many generations. Caleb left the army and joined a seminary for further training in his new faith. After graduation he was ordained into the Presbyterian ministry. The settled life of parish minister, however, was not what Caleb and Manok wanted. Missions was on their minds. There were personal reasons for this passion but there were also historical reasons for it as well.

Korean Protestantism is one of the most missions-mobilized movements in the world. Per capita, South Korean Christians send out more missionaries than any other country anywhere, and that includes the United States.[1] What were the causes of this powerful mission-minded church? One of the main causes, Caleb believes, was a revival in the Korean church that took place in the decade before World War I. For Caleb, Manok and many modern Korean Christian leaders, to understand the Korean church requires a trip back in time to the roots of indigenous Korean Protestantism in the revival of 1907.

THE BIRTH OF KOREAN PROTESTANTISM: MISSIONARY TRANSMISSION

To an observer based in New York, London or Paris, the world in 1900 seemed little more than a suburb of Europe. When Queen Victoria died on January 22, 1901, her empire covered much of Asia, Africa and the Americas. Other European sovereigns tried to follow suit. "Europeanization" circled the globe as the new century dawned. European governments managed vast colonial empires in Asia and Africa. European businesses controlled trade from Tahiti to Timbuktu. European religion, the Christianity of Christendom, seemed poised to sweep away her global religious rivals. Americans, though often regarded as Europeans with funny accents, were part of this scramble for empire. American imperial adventures in Cuba and the Philippines made clear which side of the global power divide they were on.[2]

In 1900 the rest of the world reacted violently to this suburban status. Little good did it do. On an April night in 1903 Serbian assassins bru-

---

[1]Lamin Sanneh, *Disciples of All Nations: Pillars of World Christianity* (New York: Oxford University Press, 2008), p. xxiii.

[2]J. M. Roberts, *Twentieth Century: A History of the World 1900 to the Present* (London: Penguin, 1999), pp. 847-49.

tally murdered their monarchs, Alexander and Draga, for their subservience to the Austro-Hungarian Empire and resistance to Serbian independence, throwing their mutilated bodies from a window in their Belgrade palace as a symbol of their rage against the status quo.[3] The first stirrings of nationalism appeared in India but the nation was tucked firmly under the arm of the British Raj. Chinese radicals killed converts and missionaries alike in the bloody Boxer rebellion (derived from the protestors' formal name, "The Righteous Harmonious Fist") but failed to halt the advance of the "foreign devils." Afrikaners, who saw themselves more as an African tribe than a European one, lost a savage war to Britain and faced extinction as a people. Nations like Japan were the exceptions. Rather than fighting Western progress, they embraced it. They saw clearly that survival depended on exploiting European power and technology, not resisting it. Her successful wars against China (1895) and Russia (1905) seemed to prove the point. The future faced West.

A Swahili proverb says that when elephants fight, the grass gets trampled. Though Japan cashed in on the spread of European commerce and technology, becoming one of Asia's elephants, most nations in the global South felt more like trampled grass. This was certainly true of Korea.

In the 1980s academics gave a name to this crisis faced by Korea and a host of ancient kingdoms in the global South—globalization. Today we talk about the colonialism and imperialism of 1900 as part of this larger phenomenon. Globalization, in the opinion of some, means shrinkage and sameness.[4] The world shrinks as the West draws the world into a tighter political and economic web. World culture, consequently, loses its variety as the center of power imposes its goods and its gods on a defenseless global South. The keen observer of 1900 would have had little trouble accepting this understanding of globalization.

Something strange, however, happened in Korea. A movement

---

[3]Martin Gilbert, *A History of the Twentieth Century* (New York: HarperCollins, 2001), p. 16.

[4]Anthony Giddens, *Runaway World: How Globalisation Is Reshaping Our Lives* (London: Profile Books, 1999), ably represents this widespread understanding.

emerged that would shake this understanding of globalization. An indigenous Korean Christianity was born in the fiery furnace of a globalized world and walked out of that furnace alive and well. Globalization had met its match and was permanently altered for the rest of the century. I'd like to tell the story of the rise of Korean Protestantism and its significance for understanding the paradox of globalization. That story is rooted in a global revival, the Korean Pentecost of 1907.

Christianity had come to Korea long before the twentieth century. Roman Catholic Christianity appeared in Korea in the late eighteenth century, brought by converted Korean Confucianist scholars who had been exposed to Jesuits in China. Yet despite indigenous missionaries the new teaching was regarded throughout the nineteenth century as a dangerous and foreign intrusion. Official hatred of the faith boiled over in 1866 with the massacre of some ten thousand missionaries, priests and converts.[5] With the opening up of the "Hermit Kingdom" to Western influence in the 1880s a new brand of Christianity arrived on the scene. After 1884 a steady stream of Presbyterian and Methodist missionaries appeared in Korea and began building schools, hospitals and churches.

The influence of mission strategist John Nevius was crucial to many young Presbyterian missionaries who were part of this wave. In 1886, Nevius, a Presbyterian missionary to China, published his *The Planting and Development of Missionary Churches.*[6] In this work Nevius emphasized themes that had been articulated earlier by Henry Venn and Rufus Anderson, namely the importance of planting self-governing, self-supporting and self-propagating churches. On a visit to Korea in 1890 Nevius publicized his principles and found a receptive audience among his fellow Presbyterian missionaries.[7]

---

[5]See the discussion of the origins of Korean Christianity in Vinson Synan, "The Yoido Full Gospel Church," *Cyberjournal for Pentecostal-Charsimatic Research* 2, July 1997.

[6]John L. Nevius, *The Planting and Development of Missionary Churches* (1886; reprint, Hancock, N.H.: Mt. Monadnock, 2003).

[7]Mark Noll, "Evangelical Identity, Power and Culture in the 'Great' Nineteenth Century," in *Christianity Reborn: The Global Expansion of Evangelicalism in the Twentieth Century,* ed. Donald M. Lewis (Grand Rapids: Eerdmans, 2004), p. 49.

36

There were three ways that the Nevius principles affected the early decades of Korean Protestantism. Historian Mark Noll has brought attention to two of them. First was the decision in 1893 to produce a vernacular Korean translation of the Scripture *(Hangul)*. This project built on the work done by a host of earlier missionary translators as well as pioneering Korean translator Yi Su-Jong who had produced the first vernacular translation of the Gospel of Mark in 1884.

Second was the use of *Hananim* as the name for God. This name "had factored large in Korea's historic shamanistic religion." Noll asserts that this divine name kept alive an essential contribution of shamanism—direct experience of God for healing and help in daily life—in ways that influenced subsequent Protestantism.[8] A third application of the Nevius principles, not mentioned by Noll, was the focus on education and leadership development. This was a decision that not only put Korean Christianity on the fast track toward self-government but also produced an inevitable power struggle between missionaries and Korean nationals. Ironically these three expressions of Nevius's missionary strategy produced assertive Korean converts who grew impatient with the missionary's lingering control of the new churches. Soon a struggle for control in the church mirrored the wider struggle ripping apart the nation.

In 1895 Korea became a modern nation-state, at least in name. This status was granted in the treaty that ended the Sino-Japanese war fought in the waters surrounding Korea but fought with control of the Korean land mass firmly in the mind of each antagonist. For centuries the Chinese emperors regarded Korea as a vassal state in their vast empire. The Korean royal couple were given the titles king and queen, which was regarded by China as admission of Korea's inferiority to the emperor.

After a series of brilliant naval victories, Japan forced China to sue for peace. The subsequent peace treaty granted Korea autonomy from Chinese control. On paper, Korea had joined the league of modern nation-states. But on paper it remained. The Japanese soon vied with a

---

[8]Cf. chapters three and nine of Mark Noll, *The New Shape of World Christianity* (Downers Grove, Ill.: InterVarsity Press, 2009).

new power in the region, Russia, for control of the new nation. Japan's war with Russia was fought in Manchuria and Korea off and on between 1895 and 1905. This decade-long struggle ended with another Japanese victory, an embarrassing defeat for a Russian empire that would watch helplessly as certain radical groups within the motherland would rise a decade later and attempt revolution. Japan consolidated its power over Korea by formal annexation in 1910. The imperial house of Korea was deposed. Japan ruled supreme. Dreams of independence seemed to die even as they were being born.

Even while the power of self-determination as a nation was taken from them by the colonial intrusion of Japan, the transfer of power within the church was greatly accelerated by an indigenous movement that was almost instantly given the label of the "Great Revival."

J. Edwin Orr depicts the Korean revival of 1907 as a symphony of three movements. The early prayer revival of 1903 under R. A. Hardie of Wonsan constituted phase one, following seven years of church growth from 1895 to 1902. The second phase occurred in 1906 in both northern and southern Korea. John R. Mott was astounded to speak at a meeting in Seoul in 1906 that lasted over three hours and drew a crowd of six thousand men. Some two hundred seekers stayed behind for counseling after his address. The final climactic phase began in Pyongyang in 1907. This final thrust of the revival generated a spiritual fervor that continued unabated until 1910. By the time of the "million member" crusade of 1910-1911 the full force of the Great Revival had passed.[9] Let me pass over the first two phases of revival and concentrate on the final phase.

KIL SUN JU AND THE GREAT REVIVAL OF 1907: INDIGENOUS RECEPTION

By 1906 relations between missionaries and nationals reached a new

---

[9]J. Edwin Orr, *Evangelical Awakenings in Eastern Asia* (Minneapolis: Bethany, 1975), pp. 26-27, 33.

level of animosity. The United States supported Japan's claim to Korea in the aftermath of the Russo-Japanese War. William Blair describes the atmosphere of hostility in 1906. "A violent anti-foreign, especially anti-American, storm swept over the land."[10] This tension threatened to derail plans to turn the Presbyterian Church over to Korean leaders in 1907 when the Union Christian College of Pyongyang would graduate its first seven leaders. Missionary fears peaked in 1906 as they contemplated turning the church over to men with "deadly hatred in their hearts towards those whom they regard as oppressors."[11]

The emphasis on revival opened up a new possibility for distressed Koreans. Internalizing the national humiliation of Korea, they began to explore spiritual solutions to the cultural crisis.[12] More specifically in this atmosphere of tension and remorse, Korean Christians looked to the mechanism of revival and church-based renewal for national answers.[13] Reports of worldwide revival produced a deep longing and ex-

---

[10]William Newton Blair and Bruce F. Hunt, *The Korean Pentecost and the Sufferings Which Followed* (1910; reprint, Carlisle, Penn.: Banner of Truth, 1977), p. 65.

[11]Ibid. The national humiliation of Korea deepened in 1907. Emperor Kojong had secretly appealed to the Hague without success in 1906 asking for international condemnation of Japanese occupation. Not only were his overtures rebuffed at the Hague but his action was discovered by Japan. His forced abdication was followed by the puppet regime of his son. In the same year the Korean Army was disbanded deepening the sense of national impotence. For Koreans the loss of political independence through Japanese occupation and the forced abdication of the Korean emperor were devastating. Out of rage and frustration many took to the mountains to join the "Righteous Armies" that fought the new imperialists. The Korean church contemplated its choices. Some felt keenly the call to armed struggle. The majority, however, diagnosed the national malady in different terms and refused the flight to the mountains. Most Korean Christians felt that this loss of independence was connected with their lack of Christian zeal and sincerity, a lack that the vitamin of revival might remedy.

[12]G. Lak-Chun Paik, *The History of Protestant Missions in Korea: 1832-1910*, 2nd ed. (Seoul: Yonsei University Press, 1971), p. 370.

[13]C. E. Sharp noted in 1906, that though fear may have played a role in the surge in church attendance, "owing to the uncertainty of the times," many were inspired by a larger hope. "Many," added Sharp, "are realizing the failure of the ancient civilization of their fathers, in the stress of the twentieth century." Christianity could well be a way to negotiate modernity and build a viable nation-state. On a more existential level Sharp sensed the deepest level of Christian appeal: hungry souls and the search for an alternative community. Dr. Arthur Brown's comment in 1901 describes this deeper need: "I saw how the Gospel had enlightened their hearts and how their once joyless lives now centered in the Church of God, which gave them their only light and peace" (Paik, *History*, p. 357).

pectation for a similar movement to occur in Korea. In 1906 Dr. How-
ard A. Johnston arrived in Korea and related stories of revival movements
in India and Wales. The Presbyterian missionary community was
greatly affected as they listened to tales of renewal among Welsh Presbyterians.[14] Inspired by the early revival rumblings under Hardie and
the "Bible women" of Wonsan in 1903, missionaries began to use revival methods which had proved useful elsewhere. Revival prayer,
preaching and special meetings multiplied, all calculated to produce an
awakened Korean Christianity.

The early phases of the revival reached their zenith in January 1907
during a ten-day Bible conference in Pyongyang attended by some fifteen hundred men. An evening worship service turned into a time of
extraordinary prayer and public confession. One Mr. Kang publicly
confessed his hidden hatred of the missionary who was hosting the
Bible conference, Mr. Lee. Lee, for his part, was stunned at this confession but graciously received Kang's apology.[15] With such public confession and visible reconciliation the floodgates opened wide. Lord Cecil, who witnessed the scene in Pyongyang, described it for the *London
Times* as a "poignant sense of mental anguish" due to conviction of sin.
Public confession and weeping began at eight in the evening and continued until five the next morning. The missionaries, wrote Cecil, were
"frightened by the presence of a power which could work such wonders." This pattern of all night confession and repentance continued for
several days.

William Blair describes an equally stunning phenomenon—
simultaneous prayer. "The whole audience began to pray out loud, all
together" producing an "effect that was indescribable." Remarkably the
result was "not confusion, but a vast harmony of souls and spirit, a min-
gling together of souls moved by an irresistible impulse of prayer" which
"sounded to me like the falling of many waters."[16]

<hr>

[14]Orr, *Evangelical Awakenings*, p. 27.
[15]Blair and Hunt, *Korean Pentecost*, p. 73.
[16]Paik, *History*, pp. 370-71.

The revival spread from the ten-day conference to the local theological college. Orr records that an estimated 90 percent of the students at the Union Christian College in Pyongyang "professed conversion" in February 1907, within weeks of the January outbreak of the revival.[17] In May 1907 the missionaries held special revival meetings for the students. As missionary G. S. McCune described, "These men, who are to be the pastors of Korean churches, experienced the fire of the Holy Spirit burning sin out of their lives." One of the students who played a leading role both before and during the spread of the revival to the College was Kil Sun Ju (1865-1935).[18]

Kil was twenty-one when he converted from Taoism to Christianity under the influence of missionary Samuel Moffat.[19] He joined Moffat in the work in Pyongyang and became one of the first seven Korean leaders trained at the Union Christian College who were projected to graduate in 1907 and lead the soon-to-be-formed self-governing Korean Presbyterian Church. The Japanese invasion and occupation of his homeland undoubtedly affected Kil as intensely as it did his contemporaries but under the influence of the revival he developed a different vision for Korean nationalism, a vision that had its roots in one of Kil's intellectual and spiritual mentors, Yun Chi-Ho.

Yun Chi-Ho may have been the leading influence on an entire generation of the Korean Protestant elite. He was one of the most distinguished presidents of the Independence Club, an early expression of Korean nationalism. A Confucian scholar in his own country, he traveled to America after his conversion and attended both Emory University and Vanderbilt. He became minister of education in Korea and was

---

[17]Orr, *Evangelical Awakenings*, p. 29.

[18]Quoted in Paik, *History*, p. 373. Missionaries were strategic in the early phases of the revival but Korean leadership became dominant from 1906 onward. Kil Sun Ju, Kim Ik Du and Yi Yong Do carried the message of the revival throughout the country. Between 1906 and 1910 when Korean national leaders dominated the revival an estimated eighty thousand new converts joined the churches. Kil was clearly the most prominent Korean revivalist in these crucial years.

[19]Sungjin Chang, "Korean Bible Women: Their Vital Contribution to Korean Protestantism, 1895-1945" (Ph.D. diss., University of Edinburgh, 2005), pp. 195-96.

41

instrumental in ending the grip of neo-Confucianism on the curriculum. If Kil Sun Ju was a major new light leader of the revival, Yun was a major influence on Kil Sun Ju and his generation of ardent Protestants.

Yun's concept of nationalism required spiritual renewal as a necessary precedent to political renewal. As early as the 1890s he had warned churches to avoid getting too mired in politics because it would divert the church from its primary responsibility of furthering spiritual renewal in the nation. As Yun declared, "The interest of the Kingdom of Christ cannot, and must not, be identified with the interest of a party."[20] This view was less a reflection of an American evangelical dualism than a more indigenous conviction that "societal change without this inner transformation could never achieve genuine liberation."[21] Historian Kenneth Wells labels this approach to nationalism, "self-reconstruction" nationalism. For Koreans this meant the building of a "modern nation-state whose identity centered on the attainment of a democratic, self-reliant, 'Christian' society through spiritual renewal, moral reformation and purposeful action."[22]

It is against this background that Kil's preaching and confession in January 1907 needs to be understood. During the first week of the revival not only did he preach a crucial sermon but shocked the congregation by publicly confessing to a scandalous sin. He had stolen a large amount of money from the estate of the widow of a good friend. Kil was from the Yanbon class, the scholarly elite of Korea, second only to the royal class in esteem. For him to confess publicly to the *minjung* (the masses) was the beginning of a social revolution.[23]

Kil's leadership of the Great Revival from 1907 onward needs to be seen in light of this self-reconstruction nationalism. Kil was familiar

---

[20]Kenneth Wells, *New God, New Nation: Protestants and Self-Reconstruction Nationalism in Korea 1896-1937* (Honolulu: University of Hawaii Press, 1990).

[21]Ibid.

[22]Ibid., p. viii.

[23]Caleb Chul-Soo Kim, "Confession in the Pyung-Yang Revival in 1907," *High Calling*, spring 2007.

with the missionary line on political involvement.[24] Australian Presbyterian missionaries, who were not exceptional in this regard, as part of their pre-field orientation were told that the concern of the missionary is exclusively the individual and not the society, though change in the latter may well occur because of change in the former. The watchword of the missionary was that "missions deal with the individual and through him reach society." Few missionaries would have seen this as a sufficient social theology but accepted it pragmatically as the best way to build the church without incurring the wrath of the state.[25] Kil was undoubtedly influenced by such missionary attitudes but filtered them through his own inherited tradition.

Graduation from the Union Christian College in Pyongyang in 1907 would mean not only ordination for Kil. It would also mean a new church constitution putting the Korean Presbyterian Church firmly in Korean hands. As the dream of self-rule faded in the nation, it came alive in the church. Kil's intense participation in the second phase of the revival such as the extended prayer meetings of 1906 and special meetings for the purpose of confession and reconciliation were not pietistic fiddling while his nation burned. Kil connected Korean independence with spiritual renovation.

Although he accepted much of the traditional Christian eschatology, he nonetheless filtered this doctrine through his new light vision.[26] In one of the books he wrote after his ordination Kil made clear that his concept of the gospel was not escapist but transformational. In *Malsehak* ("Teaching of the End Times") Kil envisioned Christian salvation

---

[24]The Methodist bishop, M. C. Harris, was perhaps the most outspoken missionary leader who advocated submission to Japan. But his views were not shared by all missionaries. Walter Smith, a Presbyterian missionary in North Korea wrote critically of Harris that he "is quite generally considered an agent of the Japanese government rather than a Bishop in the Christian Church" although Smith himself conceded that annexation by the Japanese would be better than the "present condition" of disorder and chaos. Paik sees more support for submission to Japanese colonialism among the missionaries than he does support for independence (Paik, *History*, pp. 414-16).

[25]Ibid., p. 41.

[26]Chung-Shin Park, *Protestantism and Politics in Korea* (Seattle: University of Washington Press, 2003), p. 61.

as "this worldly" eschatological change. "The elements of the natural world," Kil declared, "are changed by internal transformation. Accordingly, all that God creates, however small, is never destroyed, but changes its form."[27] This dramatic change of all things would be complete in the future but could be experienced now as signs of the coming kingdom. This was not the missionary party line.

Kil challenged a theological position strongly held by the resident Presbyterian missionaries in Korea—cessationism. This doctrine rejected the continuing validity of signs and wonders, phenomena that fills the New Testament record. The basis for this rejection is the completion of the New Testament. Miraculous signs were needed before the Bible was inscripturated and canonized to give authority to the early church leaders. With the death of the last apostle, however, the extraordinary signs and wonders gives way to the regular teaching and preaching of the written Word. Kil challenged cessationism. His eschatology taught that the kingdom of God comes not only at the end of time but in the midst of time. The strong implication was that the in-breaking of the kingdom now would be through remarkable signs and wonders such as the revival of 1907. Rather than seeking such movements as extraordinary, Kil implied that the visitation of kingdom powers should be a regular experience of the faithful church.

What Kil proclaimed, Ik Doo Kim demonstrated. Ik Doo Kim's healing ministry which grew out of the revival pressed home the new paradigm that Kil preached. Traveling from village to village during the years of Japanese occupation, Kim conducted a ministry of healing, exorcism and other miracles. For Kil the ministry of Kim confirmed his kingdom eschatology. For the missionaries the ministry of signs and wonders contradicted much of what they were trying to do in Korea. Some missionaries denounced the work of Ik Doo Kim as anarchic and subversive to the real work of the gospel. Other missionaries and

---

[27]Chang, "Korean Bible Women," p. 196.

most of the Korean converts were less certain of this criticism.

A commission was created to investigate the miracles carefully to determine their authenticity. The results of that investigation were eventually published in 1923 as the *Certificate of Miracles.* Much to Presbyterian surprise the report validated the genuineness of Kim's signs and wonders. As a result of this report the bylaws of the church were changed to remove the phrase in article one of chapter three: "the power of doing miracles had ceased at the present time."[28] A powerful paradigm shift had taken place that would characterize and sustain Korean Christian throughout the century.

After 1907 Kil spread the new light of the Christian gospel and its role in self-reconstruction nationalism throughout the country. From 1907 to 1919 he was the most visible face of the new revived Korean Christianity. His opposition to Korean Christians joining the Righteous Armies (which were quickly obliterated by the Japanese) is less a sign of his American "fundamentalism" than his commitment to an alternative nationalism. "The emphasis on personal salvation," Wells concludes, "did not deprive the early Korean Christians of a social philosophy."

Though the fires of revival cooled after 1910, Kil's dream of a visible Christian nationalism that anticipated the coming kingdom of Christ never faded. In 1919 he was one of a courageous group of Korean leaders to sign the Korean Declaration of Independence which called for the end of colonial control and the restoration of an autonomous and independent Korea.[29] Kil put his life on the line again in 1935 when he protested Japan's imposition of Shintoism in Korea and died a martyr's death.

At the famous Edinburgh missionary conference of 1910, the revival in Korea was hailed as a "genuine Pentecost," largely for the remarkable church growth that it inspired. But other consequences were less celebrated. The Korean church became self-supporting during the revival. It also saw the emergence of new Korean leadership whose participation

---

[28]Stanley M. Burgess and Eduard M. Van Der Maas, eds., *The New International Dictionary of Pentecostal and Charismatic Movements,* rev. ed. (Grand Rapids: Zondervan, 2002), p. 240.
[29]Wells, *New God,* p. 100.

in the revival gave them a spiritual validity that hastened formal ordination. When the smoke had cleared, three hundred thousand Korean Christians stood where only a handful had stood two decades before.[30]

Three hundred thousand may seem like a large number, but in Korean terms it is nothing extraordinary. After the double trauma of World War II and the Korean War of 1950 to 1953, South Korea, now divided from its northern half at the 38th parallel, underwent another spiritual crisis. Korea was caught up in right-wing dictatorships at home and the machinations of American Cold War politics abroad. Out of the crucible of this new wave of globalization came a second wave of revivals epitomized in the career of David Yongii Cho, who by the end of the century was the pastor of the largest church in the world, the seven-hundred-thousand Yoido Full Gospel Church just outside of Seoul.[31]

Cho's own conversion from shamanism and Buddhism took place during a time of prayer on a mountain. A confrontation with the world of the Spirits led to the conviction that Christ was Lord. He began his church with a handful of followers. Like Kil Sun Ju he challenged the previous paradigm of Korean Protestantism, a church-type support of the government against communism, and called for a more charismatic- and kingdom-oriented gospel that would heal individuals, families and the nation. His new paradigm attracted both the masses as well as critics.

Architects of the *minjung* (people's) theology, a form of Latin American liberation theology contextualized for Korea, wrote off Cho as just another example of an escapist right-wing evangelicalism. What actually happened was something different. Cho's paradigm began to grow to include a strong liberationist element but still centered upon the role of the Spirit as the great healer. To the modern cessasionists of political theology who overemphasize the human factor in societal change, Cho

---

[30]Orr, *Evangelical Awakenings*, pp. 69-70.
[31]Cf. the discussion of this church in Alan Anderson, *Introduction to Pentecostalism* (Cambridge: Cambridge University Press, 2004).

restored the vision of Kil Sun Ju that the kingdom breaks into time in ways that do not neatly fit into the categories of the left or the right. When political theologian Jürgen Moltmann stood in the pulpit of Cho's full gospel church to declare that he had been healed under the ministry of Cho and that Cho's charismatic gospel actually was a potent synthesis of liberation theology and charismatic power, few doubted that another Korean Pentecost had come.[32]

REVIVAL, GLOBALIZATION AND GLOCALIZATION

The Korean revival of 1907 is a clear example of the kind of indigenous movement I am calling a global revival. Historically Korean Christians entered a problem phase during the colonization by Japan. Every institution of Korean life was shaken by this event. Missionary leadership, dominated by Americans, was called into question when American foreign policy supported Japan's imperial claims on Korea. While some Korean Christians took to the mountains as rebels, those who stayed within the mission churches sought a third way between missionary Christianity and a return to a militant Korean nationalism. Kil Sun Ju emerged as a new light leader, someone who underwent a profound renewal and who subsequently cast a new theological vision influenced by his experience. Korean Presbyterians in particular were dramatically changed by the new paradigm that expected the in-breaking of the kingdom into contemporary Korean life. In the power stage that began in the second decade of the twentieth century, Korean Protestants played a key role in leading Korean Protestantism into a form of civil society that provided an alternative nationalism during the years of Japanese occupation. It is significant that Kil Sun Ju and several other Protestant leaders were among those who signed the declaration of Korean independence in 1919. Ardent Protestants like Kil sealed their new light leadership with a martyr's death in the 1930s, but not before

---

[32]Jürgen Moltmann, "The Blessing of Hope: The Theology of Hope and the Full Gospel of Life," *Journal of Pentecostal Theology* 13 (2005): 147-61.

helping to lead Korean Christianity into several decades of advance through the storm.

There are a number of features of the revival of 1907 that could be analyzed but the one element I'd like to look at is that of globalization and its offspring, glocalization.

Korea is the poster child of globalization. The authors of *Exporting the American Gospel*, for example, state that Korea "has undergone a one-hundred-year period of modernization—culturally, economically and politically—that has been as complete, and maybe as ruthless, as anywhere on earth."[33] Korea has been a cultural chessboard upon which the forces of capitalism, communism, indigenous religion and Western Christianity have clashed. Keeping stride with this century of modernization, Korean Christianity has grown explosively and become one of the most vital expressions of the faith in Asia and beyond. Such an ideal cultural laboratory for examining the impact of globalization on Christianity should not be missed. As Peter Berger suggested, just as "an art collector would naturally be drawn to Florence," and "a mountain climber to the Himalayas," so too should a social scientist interested in globalization "have his attention fixed on East Asia."[34]

Was the Great Revival of 1907 evidence of an exported American missionary Christianity that manhandled Korean traditional religion and culture? Susan Rose thinks so. She sees the Korean revival as reactionary and counterproductive. Though Protestant Christianity in the 1890s and early 1900s had inspired new nationalistic movements, the 1907 revival was "intentionally inaugurated by the missionaries to counteract specific nationalist uprising."[35] The tone of Korean Protestantism was now set: "emotional, conservative, Pentecostal, individualistic and other-worldly."

Jung Young Lee sees the revival of 1907 as an expression of "pietistic

---

[33]Steve Brouwer, Paul Gifford and Susan D. Rose, *Exporting the American Gospel: Global Christian Fundamentalism* (New York: Routledge, 1996), p. 112.
[34]Ibid.
[35]Ibid.

fundamentalism." Lee identifies Kil Sun Ju as the leading exemplar of this otherworldly faith. For Lee, Kil is a champion of Christian dualism with its "radical separation of inner and outer, the secular and the religious, the church and the state." As part of this dualism, Kil and revival Christianity "encouraged personal salvation rather than social and political justice." From this perspective, Protestant revivalism not only prevented any true inculturation of Christian faith in Korea but also rendered it impotent before the powerful globalizing forces of Japanese colonialism before World War II and of capitalistic neo-colonialism after the war.[36]

There is another way, however, to understand the 1907 revival and the kind of Christianity it produced. Roland Robertson is one of the pioneering thinkers in the area of globalization.[37] Over the last twenty years he has tweaked his understanding of this important concept in important ways.

How does a religion spin the secular straw of globalization into the gold of revitalized faith and practice? Robertson's answer is *glocalization*. In a series of perceptive studies Robertson explores the paradox of cultural globalization: It can both threaten and revitalize local culture.[38] Robertson agrees that globalization's most obvious face is "the compression of the world." He also agrees that the process of compressing the world is not a recent development but has spanned several centuries.

A second aspect of globalization is "homogenization"—the spread of certain Western brands of goods and services on a global basis. Robertson accepts that "shrinkage" and "sameness" are real aspects of globalization. What he does not accept is that they are the whole story.[39]

---

[36]Jung Young Lee, "Korean Theology," in *The Blackwell Encyclopedia of Modern Christian Thought,* ed. Alister E. McGrath (Oxford: Blackwell, 1993).

[37]Habibul Haque Khondker, "Glocalization as Globalization: Evolution of a Sociological Concept," *Bangladesh e-Journal of Sociology* 1, no. 2 (July 2004).

[38]Roland Robertson, *Globalization: Social Theory and Global Culture,* Theory, Culture & Society (London: Sage, 1992); Roland Robertson, "Globalization and the Future of 'Traditional Religion,'" in *God and Globalization,* ed. Max Stackhouse (Harrisburg, Penn.: Trinity Press International, 2000).

[39]Robertson, "Globalization," pp. 53-56.

Robertson draws attention to the wider category of culture. On this level globalization moves in two directions. The modernizing forces of globalization cruise along the global freeway at high speeds but passing it in the other direction is a long caravan of local traditions and cultures heading west. "Globalization," says Robertson "has encouraged tradition" and accelerated "the promotion of traditional culture." Robertson cites the World's Parliament of Religions in Chicago in 1893 as evidence. Gathered at this unprecedented event were particular religions each with a traditional heartland and culture but now globalized by being presented as "world religions."[40] Prior to the parliament many of these "world religions" were regional faiths little understood in the West. As a result of the parliament, a globalizing cultural event, the local becomes the global. He calls this renewal and revitalization of the local glocalization. Robertson gives due credit to the Japanese business term, *dochakuka*—global localization—as his inspiration. Glocalization for Robertson does not negate globalization but it does limit its homogenizing tendencies. In reality "globalization and localization proceed in tandem." For Robertson the future is about a "world of difference within sameness."[41]

It would be pleasant to think glocalization occurs painlessly. The reality is quite different. The resurgence of the local grows out of a traumatic process Robertson calls relativization. Global cultural forces produce a local culture shock, a feeling of being a stranger in one's own homeland. The volatility that arises from this culture shock inspires various attempts to "save" one's culture or tradition. Various "fundamentalisms" have been identified (an American conservative Christian in the 1920s, an Islamist Iranian in the 1970s) to illustrate the angry reactions to such threats. In one sense then, globalization tends to produce a strident antiglobalism or globaphobia alongside its diffusion of international values and products. Globalization, however, does not have to lead "automatically to a more violent or conflict-filled world."

---

[40]Ibid., pp. 58-59.
[41]Ibid., p. 61.

Robertson is hopeful that people will learn to deal more constructively with the forces of relativization. Local renewal may produce creative engagement instead of angry reaction. As new value is placed on "locality, home and community" after the confrontation with globalizing forces, the local tradition can gain new confidence and develop a new sense of mission and global relevance. In this light "the local is best seen as a global phenomenon." Continuous cultural renewal is possible in such a global climate. For this reason "the future of traditional culture and religion is bright."[42]

If *glocalization* describes the *fact* of local renewal, *revivals* describe an important *force* behind the fact. Operating under a wide variety of names (revivals, revitalization movement, evangelical renewal, awakenings, indigenous movements, new religious movements, to name but a few), global revivals often represent "people power" in the face of globalizing tendencies. These movements "from below" have the capacity to interact with outside cultural, political or economic forces and empower local groups to adapt to the new forces. Global revivals have the power to take what is alien and transform it into the indigenous.

The paradox of globalization, that the secular flood of cultural imports actually produces a new harvest of local religious vitality, must now be seen to be a key external factor in the rise of world Christianity. "The most obvious, most salient, and most powerful cause of the global religious resurgence," writes political scientist Samuel Huntington, "is precisely what was supposed to cause the death of religion: the processes of social, economic, and cultural modernization that swept across the world in the second half of the twentieth century." Huntington sees the current global revival of religion as "a reaction against secularism, moral relativism, and self-indulgence and a reaffirmation of the values of order, discipline, work, mutual help and human solidarity."[43] Religion, therefore, for much of the world is not "the opium of the people

---

[42]Ibid., p. 66.
[43]Samuel P. Huntington, *The Clash of Civilizations and the Remaking of World Order* (New York: Simon & Schuster, 1966), p. 98.

but the vitamin of the weak."[44] I am not arguing that global forces explain the Korean revival. I am arguing that Korean Protestantism illustrates how global dynamics act as framework for other dynamics (spiritual, cultural, historical and group) that create global revivals.

The Great Revival of 1907 was not only a movement of missionary inspired church growth. I have argued in this chapter that the *Korean Revival of 1907 transformed Korean Protestantism by turning globalization (the transmission of alien commerce, culture and religion) into glocalization (indigenous reception and expansion of the localized faith)*. I have further suggested that this external dynamic is a common feature in twentieth-century global revivals in general. I believe the remaining case studies in this book will bear this out. The Korean revival reminds us that World Christianity, as Lamin Sanneh observes, "is not merely an echo of globalization" but rather a creative "laboratory of pluralism and diversity where instead of faith and trust being missing or compromised, they remain intrinsic."[45]

Caleb and Manok returned to South Korea in 2007, the centenary of the Great Revival. Everywhere they turned they saw churches celebrating the event with the banners "Do it again." Caleb has his doubts how seriously Korean Christians take this prayer. Caleb admits that though the churches may sincerely want the growth and vitality that global revival brings, he wonders whether they are willing to pay the price of alienation, humiliation and radical repentance that were the preconditions of 1907. Perhaps the very concern of many Christians in Korea is a sign of hope.

South Korean Christianity is feeling another strong wave of globalization. Korean youth seem more attuned to technology and American pop culture than to theology and public confession. Once again the

---

[44]Ibid., p. 101.
[45]Lamin Sanneh, *Whose Religion Is Christianity? The Gospel Beyond the West* (Grand Rapids: Eerdmans, 2003), p. 75. Mark Noll's important thesis in *The New Shape of World Christianity* is relevant here. Noll argues that the most important influence of American-style Protestantism was not through direct importation but rather the indirect influence of similar conditions such as pluralism, volunteerism and revivalism. Cf. Noll, *New Shape*, pp. 162-68.

winds of secularization that so threatened the vitality of Korean Protestantism in the early twentieth century are blowing again at the dawn
of the twenty-first. The paradox of globalization, like the paradox of
Good Friday leading to Easter Sunday, may yet be the prelude for another great awakening.

The leadership of Kil Sun Ju was also a crucial factor in the Korean
revival. This leadership factor warrants closer examination. The African prophets of Aladura in the West Africa of the 1930s and 1940s
provide one of the best case studies of revival leadership in action.

3

THE RESURRECTION MAN

Joseph Babalola and
the Aladura Revival of 1930

He looks out at us from the grainy black and white photograph like an African Moses. His full white and gray beard, small dark eyes framed by a thick brow, lips parted as though about to speak, robe and turban bleached a blinding white, and small Ethiopian cross hanging slightly askew around his neck, all announce that this is a man on a mission. He is not Joseph Babalola, the subject of this chapter. He is William Wade Harris, Liberian evangelist and prototypical African Christian prophet, a John the Baptist figure for all the Babalolas that were to follow. Prophet Harris is a fitting entree into the strange and wonderful world of AICs (African Initiated Churches) and the revival movements that create them. "When the full story of the creation of a Christian people in Africa will be told by Africans," wrote David Shank, "the chapter on their prophets will be an important one."[1] Harris was the most successful Protestant missionary in West Africa before World War II. The fact that he is an African missionary from Liberia underscores the importance of his story.

Imprisoned during the Glebo war in Liberia in 1910 (for agitating

---

[1]David A. Shank, *Prophet Harris, the "Black Elijah" of West Africa* (Leiden: E. J. Brill, 1994), p. xi.

for the overthrow of Americo-Liberians), Harris was visited by the angel Gabriel. He was given a new identity as the last Elijah and told to preach a message of radical monotheism, repentance, the destruction of fetishes and baptism. After his release from prison he traveled to what is now the Ivory Coast and Ghana. By one estimate the number of people who accepted his gospel and abandoned African traditional religion may have approached two hundred thousand. After his death, these converts found their way into Methodist, Baptist and Roman Catholic churches as well as founding their own independent Harrist Church.[2]

Harris is important for our purposes not only because of his personal success as a missionary evangelist but also because he typifies so many of the new light leaders and their AICs that dominate African Christianity before independence. When David Barrett wrote about these movements in the 1960s he had identified some six thousand of them. More recent figures estimate their number to be closer to ten thousand.[3]

I have been intrigued by AICs ever since arriving in Kenya in 1980. Though the great day of these churches had passed, the presence of AICs were everywhere in my little town an hour outside of Nairobi. The African Brotherhood church, the African Israel Church Nineveh, the Mario Legio, to name but a few, were all around me. They paraded to their churches, built new buildings, marched, drummed, healed and preached their recovery of Christian faith from the clutches of foreign captivity. Some of their sons and daughters even found their way into my classes. Only gradually did I realize that AICs are not just an interesting sideline to "mainline" Christianity but in fact with some ninety-five million adherents (1995) may well be the real mainline.[4]

I slowly became interested in the story behind the rise of this large host of churches. More often than not, at the heart of their story was a

---

[2]Ibid.; cf. chapter one for a summary of his missionary work.
[3]Erwin Fahlbusch et al., *Encyclopedia of Christianity* (Grand Rapids: Eerdmans, 1999), 1:30.
[4]Alan Anderson and Edmond Tang, "Independency in Africa and Asia," in *The Cambridge History of Christianity: World Christianity c.1914–c.2000,* The Cambridge History of Christianity (Cambridge: Cambridge University Press, 2007), p. 115.

renewal movement. In case after case, at the heart of these revivals, was a prophetic leader. Afe Adogame has written that "virtually all the AICs trace their emergence to a charismatic, prophetic figure usually with claims of a traumatic religious experience."[5] In this chapter, I'd like to examine the role of leadership in global revivals using not Harris's movement but the Babalola revival of 1930 that lies at the chronological and spiritual heart of the Aladura churches of Nigeria, churches that in the last few decades have spread around the world. I'd like to explore the important role that such leaders play in making Christianity indigenous, that is shifting power from missionary leadership to local leadership. As we will see, this power transfer normally happens when the prophet sees the gospel in a new light, a light that shows an enslaved people a new way to the promised land.

Our quest to understand revival leadership focuses on Joseph Babalola, the resurrection man, and his powerful gospel paradigm that helped ignite one of the greatest mass movements of the twentieth century in Africa.

BACKGROUND OF THE REVIVAL

The Babalola revival must be seen against the backdrop of fear and plague which swept over southern Nigeria in the mid- to late-1920s. Between 1924 and 1926 Lagos suffered with an epidemic bubonic plague. So dangerous was the situation that the visit of the Prince of Wales to Nigeria in April of 1925 was postponed. As the plague swept into the rural areas panic mounted. In the village of Ogere, the birthplace of another key Aladura prophet, Josiah Oshitelu, an observer wrote that the plague had so infected the population that "there are no voices in many parts to be heard save the deep groanings of the bereaved." The influenza epidemic of 1918 also affected thousands in Ni-

---

[5]Afe Adogame and Lizo Jafta, "Zionists, Aladura and Roho: African Instituted Churches," in *African Christianity: An African Story,* ed. Ogbu Kalu (Pretoria, South Africa: University of Pretoria, 2005), p. 319.

geria as did the world economic depression of 1930.[6] For many it seemed
the world might be coming to end, so violent were these tremors. This
is a description of large-scale cultural distortion. Volatility was everywhere. The Western system of fighting evil (colonial administration,
modern medicine and education) appeared impotent against the rav-
ages of influenza, war, plague and economic depression. The gods, old
and new, seemed to have failed. A new Moses was needed to lead the
people out of darkness.[7]

One of the notable features of the prevalent African Yoruba religion
at the time was its "this-worldly" orientation, with its *orisa* (deities who
control daily life). Those who followed Yoruba wanted a religion and a
god that did something, someone who could deliver the goods of daily
life, such as a healthy birth, a fertile marriage and a bounteous crop.
They were not looking for "personal peace and happiness" so much as
they were looking for a world in which evil, that which destroys life,
has been conquered.[8]

The Yoruba had joined Christian churches in large numbers during the
period before 1890. By 1920 many were disillusioned with missionary
Christianity. Missionary paternalism didn't help. Foreign monopoly of
leadership proved frustrating to talented Christian converts.[9]

Deeper however than the struggle for church power was the struggle
for divine power. Between 1910 and 1920 prophets like Egunjobi and
Moses Orimolade wandered through Yoruba land challenging the
power of ancient fetishes and modern medicine. The great influenza

[6]This pandemic, estimated to have taken some twenty million lives worldwide continues to be
the subject of medical research and debate. A medical researcher at Emory University now
claims that it was strep bacteria and not flu that was the true cause of the epidemic. Cf. "Bacteria, not flu, cause of 1918 pandemic (ABC News in Science)," <www.abc.net.au/science/
articles/2009/02/06/2484125.htm?site=science&topic=latest>.
[7]Robert Cameron Mitchell, "Religious Protest and Social Change: The Origins of the aladura
Movement in Western Nigeria," in *Protest and Power in Black Africa,* ed. Robert Rotberg and
Ali Al'Amin Mazrui (New York: Oxford University Press, 1970), pp. 474-82.
[8]See the discussion of evil as that which corrupts life and health in Mark Shaw, *The Kingdom
of God in Africa: A Short History of African Christianity* (Grand Rapids: Baker, 1996). See also
Robin Horton, "African Conversion," *Africa* 41 (1971): 86.
[9]Ibid., p. 87.

epidemic that killed so many millions worldwide and tens of thousands
locally proved their point that both science and the spirits had failed.
New power, they argued, came through direct prayer to the high God,
Olurun (or Oludumare), the Creator God of the Bible. The high God
now called for the Yoruba to become a "people of prayer."

THE RISE OF BABALOLA

Joseph Babalola (1904-1959) was a young Yoruba road builder for the
colonial government when he received a call to preach the gospel. His
call was preceded by a week of intense struggle in which he was unable
to sleep. "I did not fell sleeping [*sic*]," he later wrote, "for a complete
week both day and night." Yet in this midst of this turmoil "I was happy
. . . reading books from evening to day break." He read through the
book of Psalms on a daily basis. "I did not feel sickly," he wrote, but
admitted that despite these spiritual exertions, "I saw nothing."[10] Babalola sought the council of David Odubanjo, leader of the Diamond
Society of Faith Tabernacle, an AIC begun in 1920. Odubanjo appreciated the young man's gifts and zeal and invited Babalola to a conference
of the church in 1930 in Oke-Oye, Ilesha, near Ibadan, Nigeria.[11]

According to one account, Babalola was asked by a distraught parent
to pray over her dead child. The child reportedly returned to life. Word
spread. Large crowds gathered to hear Babalola preach and to drink
"holy" water which the prophet had blessed. The Nigerian *Daily Times*
wrote in August 1930 that a prophet "is said to have put up an appear-
ance at Ilesha, whose power of healing by prayer has been testified by
many who have been healed." The news story went on to give some
specifics. "Two well-known figures in Ibadan who have nearly lost their
sights [sic] have completely recovered."[12]

Babalola's prediction of an impending world disaster prompted mass
conversions. Even the local king joined the Faith Tabernacle to escape

---

[10]Mitchell, "Religious Protest," p. 473.
[11]Ibid.
[12]Ibid., p. 474.

the wrath of God. The great indigenous appeal of Babalola was deliverance from the power of evil. "Babalola offered deliverance from sickness and the powers of evil—defined as evil spirits and witchcraft."[13]

The Babalola revival played an important role in the growth and expansion of many of the AICs collectively known as the Aladura churches. In 1930, just as the revival was beginning, Babalola met Josiah Oshitelu who, after a series of visions, had begun his own public preaching in 1929. Oshitelu emphasized witch accusation, the use of "holy words" and symbols given by direct revelation, healing and dreams. Late in 1930 he published three booklets that prophesied the coming judgment on the land in 1931 and the in-breaking of the kingdom of Christ. In what he regarded as a fulfillment of his prophecy Oshitelu founded the Church of the Lord (Aladura) in 1931. Together with Babalola's Christ Apostolic Church and the Cherubim and Seraphim, Oshitelu's Church of the Lord (Aladura) became the third strand of the historic mother churches of the Aladura movement. As the entire Aladura movement has developed each of these three churches has spread throughout West Africa and into Europe.

NEW LIGHT BREAKS

How did Babalola explain his power to raise the dead and heal? The young prophet proclaimed a message of primal Christianity as the way forward for Nigeria. Power gave Babalola credibility. But it was the paradigm of the gospel that gave Babalola power. Babalola's power to heal and to detect witches indicated that he had access to the "real" world of spiritual power.

Mitchell summarizes the message of Babalola under five headings. First, healing and protection against evil spirits comes from the Christian God. Secondly, idols and charms have no power. Third, the wrath of God will be poured out on towns that practiced or permitted adultery and witchcraft. Fourth, only repentance can avert the wrath of

---

[13]Ibid., p. 473.

God. Finally, repentance must involve confession of sins, renunciation of idols and charms, and the drinking of sacred water for healing and protection. Many of these themes have the ring of John the Baptist, the second Elijah, in preparing for the in-breaking of the rule of God directly over God's people.[14]

The revival aroused opposition. As the movement grew a number of other revival prophets not directly connected to Babalola preached against taxation and colonial injustice. Following the revival Babalola's sudden popularity so alarmed colonial authorities that they arrested him. Babalola was eventually tried and convicted for witch accusation. He was jailed for six months. Oshitelu had numerous brushes with colonial officials, particularly over his writings.

Yet the Aladura movement grew. Babalola became the head of the Christ Apostolic Church in the early thirties although the name itself was not adopted until 1943. Many of these Aladura churches continue to expand throughout West Africa, the wider continent and even Europe. The vigor of these movements is not measured only by the numbers but by the vigor of their missions which have added yet one more "I" word to the AIC acronym—*international*.[15]

GLOBAL REVIVALS AND THE TRANSFER OF POWER: THE DYNAMIC OF INDIGENIZATION

Harold Turner, one of the pioneering figures in the study of new religious movements concluded, after a lifetime of studying thousands of such movements, that the key cause was almost always "the emergence of a charismatic individual to provide a crystallizing point for an incipient movement that will otherwise never surface into history."[16]

The Aladura case study underscores Turner's point. Without revival

---

[14]Ibid., pp. 475-76.

[15]Cf. Afe Adogame, *Celestial Church of Christ: The Politics of Cultural Identity in a West African Prophetic Charismatic Movement* (Frankfurt am Main: Peter Lang, 1999).

[16]Ulrich Berner, "Reflections upon the Concept of 'New Religious Movement,'" in *Perspectives on Method and Theory in the Study of Religion*, ed. Armin W. Geertz and Russell T. McCutcheon (Leiden: Brill, 2000), pp. 268-69.

leaders there are no revival movements. When a power shift occurs from missionary transmitters to indigenous agents, local Christians often experience renewal and resurgence in life and witness. Indigenization is the missiological name for this transfer of power. Since the days of Henry Venn who called for self-governing churches, the dream of indigenous leaders has been crucial to the World Christian movement. Yet missionaries do not always give up power easily or quickly. The transfer of power sometimes requires convulsive people movements to rearrange the patterns of leadership. At the heart of these indigenous movements and the recalculating of the power equation stands the prophet. The essential tool of the power shift is not the rifle, the purse or even that ill-defined quality called charisma but the proclamation of a powerful paradigm. In revivals it is the message that makes the man.

Prophet Harris illustrates this point about the power of paradigm in granting spiritual authority to the new light leader. "Harris as prophet taught a fairly straight message about God and Christ as vanquishing and replacing the spirit of tradition."[17] But this message was not just slavish repetition of missionary proclamation. Harris's vision of the kingdom breaking into history made traditional doctrine come alive for himself and his hearers. "Harris was proclaiming the imminent return of Christ, which was to be prepared for by a radical conversion of life." This eschatological vision, however, came alive for Harris through the heavenly encounter in the darkest hours of his prison experience. He was transformed by the gospel of a victorious Jesus who not only forgives sins but transforms his world. "His visions," notes Hastings, "had provided the biblical message with a greater immediacy."[18]

The Aladura message echoed many of the same themes that Harris had proclaimed. Babalola's illness and intense week of Bible reading and prayer in which he went without sleep or food produced a live orthodoxy that not only persuaded minds but produced powerful signs.

[17]Adrian Hastings, *The Church in Africa, 1450-1950*, Oxford History of the Christian Church (Oxford: Clarendon Press, 1994), pp. 444-45.
[18]Ibid.

Anthropology confirms the power of the paradigm. Anthony Wallace, who spent his life studying Native American revitalization movements became convinced that the key factor in such movements is the rise of a visionary who is able to redraw the cultural map for a group who keep hitting dead ends and broken links following traditional mental and moral maps. This new leader emerges in the midst of what many feel are the death throes of the society. He or she possesses new light, a vision of the way forward like a Moses crossing the Red Sea.

How does the power of the Christian paradigm explain the emergent leadership of a Harris, a Babalola or an Oshitelu? Didn't missionaries preach the same gospel? Robin Horton might help us make the connection. Horton describes the Yoruba worldview in terms of the microcosm of spirits who control the world of daily life and the macrocosm of the high God separated from daily life by the world of the spirits. The crisis of plague and colonial intrusion shook the microcosm of the Yoruba world. For traditionalist or nominal Anglican alike the old way of doing things no longer worked. For new light prophets, however, this did not lead to discouragement but to a new discovery. The breakdown of the microcosmic control of the *orisa* spirits meant that the macrocosmic world of the high God had broken through. God was now taking direct control of daily life. The personal crisis gave one a new sense of sin and of God breaking in with his grace and love.

A great shift had taken place from a world of rejected orphans to the kingdom of God and a new status as much loved children. The eschatological vision meant that God would bring about not just little adjustments to reality but would instead transform the world. The power to heal or persuade others was simply an outward sign that the macrocosmic kingdom had broken through the old powers of this world. The call to repent and believe was a call to enter this new world of divine power and to expose oneself and one's family to the new possibilities and power now available.[19]

---

[19]Horton, "African Conversion."

Wherever global revival breaks out some expression of this personal crisis and eschatological vision occurs, albeit in a wide variety of cultural idioms. New light leaders trigger the revival by showing and telling their hearers that the old microcosmic powers have been broken and the new rule of the macrocosm of the kingdom has come.

THE REVIVAL LEADER AS RATIONAL ACTOR

What does this teach us about global revivals and the men and women who lead them? We are arguing in this book that revivals are both human and divine dramas in which large numbers of indigenous people change their world through the creative use of early Christianity. It is the last phrase that needs to attract our attention as we think of the role of a new light leader. It takes a Babalola, a Harris, a Whitefield or an Edwards to creatively reenvision and reapply the dynamics of early Christianity to their particular situation. Anthropologists call it the "transforming dream" (Wallace), Pentecostals "the full gospel" and evangelical theologians "live orthodoxy."

The typical revival leader is not a half-crazed Elmer Gantry. There is a fundamental rationality to the leader of a global revival. They are explorers and mapmakers of the undiscovered country of eternity. Max Weber's portrait of the charismatic leader that has done so much to shape modern understanding of revival leadership is not very helpful at this point. Many who read Weber interpret charismatic leaders as enthusiastic entertainers, dangerous manipulators or irrational lunatics.

According to the analysis of Horton, revival leaders are more often than not charismatic intellectuals who discover new maps of reality and share those maps with spiritually and culturally stranded exiles. They see a new reality that others do not see but that is verified in newly translated sacred Scriptures that reveal the omniscient mind of God. This new map of reality resolves both personal crises (such as guilt, shame and fear) while at the same time restoring hope through a new vision of a positive future (eschatological vision). Based on this ultimate rationality from above they then seek to show and proclaim what rational behavior is required in light of the new facts of existence. People who now think and live in light of these new facts become change agents in their personal worlds. Social, economic and even political change is not far behind.

From the perspective of global revivals the Aladura evangelists were tapping into a characteristically Christian way to challenge the status quo. As Ellis and Ter Haar remind us where "people aspire to communicate with an invisible world, control of such communication can become a matter of the greatest political importance."[20] To circumvent the colonial system through direct experience of the power of the kingdom of God through healing and divine approval through repentance has political implications. To declare the supremacy of the divine kingdom when other voices declared explicitly or implicitly that the state was lord is to make a political statement that calls for radical change. If politics is a matter of "who gets what, when and how," then politics will be altered in time by the new maps of the prophets. With the Babalola revival the old order has not been replaced so much as transcended.[21] That is the great secret and the great power of new light leaders in global revivals.

How does this indigenization, understood as the transfer of power from old light leaders to new light leaders, turn into a mass movement? Another dynamic is at play when we move from leadership to followership. To understand how personal visions become public movements we need help from the case of the Dornakal revival under Bishop V. S. Azariah, a new light leader among the Dalits in pre-independence India. To this revival and the great struggle over conversion that it generated we now turn.

---

[20]Stephen Ellis and Gerrie Ter Haar, *Worlds of Power: Religious Thought and Political Practice in Africa* (Oxford: Oxford University Press, 2004), p. 14.
[21]Ibid.

4

WAKING THE DEAD

V. S. Azariah and the Dornakal Revival in India

The figure of Mahatma ("Great Soul") Gandhi is hard to mistake. This great warrior in the struggle to end European colonialism in India is armed in his photographs with only a walking stick. His uniform is a homespun shawl and dhoti (a long cloth wrapped around the hips and thighs) not that of a general with medals. His arms and legs seem impossibly thin. The only thing large about the man are his wire-rimmed glasses that seem to cover half his shaven head. Yet Gandhi was diminutive only on the outside. We know from history that his inner man was possessed by an indominatable will power and bottomless self-sacrifice.

Picturing the tranquil Gandhi ruffled and annoyed is difficult. Few could break the spiritual calm that seemed to pervade the unflappable Gandhi. One of the few who could is a figure largely forgotten to history. For Gandhi, however, he won the dubious distinction of being called by the Mahatma his "number one enemy." The object of Ghandi's implacable dislike was V. S. Azariah, a mild-mannered Anglican bishop of Indian descent. In another lifetime they might have been friends.

In the turbulent decade of the 1930s as India pushed for independence they were divided by one of the most controversial issues facing the nationalists of India, the problem of Christian conversion. Azariah and Gandhi were separated by a great revival among India's impoverished Dalit class ("forsaken ones"). Dalits (also called Scheduled Castes, untouchables, outcastes or Harijan, or "Children of God" to Gandhi) numbering in the tens of thousands had converted to Christianity during a decade of evangelistic campaigns led by the Bishop. The prospect of even greater mass conversions to come infuriated Gandhi, endangering as it did his campaign to present a united Hindu front to the British in the struggle for independence. In 1938 an American missionary writing about mass movements of conversion among the Dalit in India created a national incident that threatened Hindu-Christian relations. In the final installment of a three-part article entitled "The Battle for Brotherhood in India Today," Donald A. McGavran, later of church-growth-theory fame, reported a heated exchange between nationalist leader Mohandas Gandhi, Anglican Bishop V. S. Azariah and Methodist missionary researcher J. W. Pickett:

> "We shall not allow conversions to continue," Mr. Gandhi explained in conclusion of a three-hour conference. The Christian leaders pointed out to Mr. Gandhi the unquestioned improvement which had come to the oppressed classes of people who became Christians, and tried in every way to induce him to say that he was in favour of any amelioration of their lot. But his position remained adamant, namely that it was better for the oppressed classes to suffer in Hinduism than to be relieved in Christianity. . . . At the conclusion of the conference, Mr. Gandhi said to Bishop Azariah, "You Christians must stop preaching to and making disciples amongst the Depressed Classes. If you do not, we shall make you."[1]

Gandhi was outraged by the article and demanded an apology. Azariah "responded vehemently" in the church periodical, *Guardian*, saying that "every statement—without exception—attributed to Gandhiji by Dr. MacGavran [*sic*] is wholly and absolutely untrue." The mission-

---

[1]Susan Harper, *In the Shadow of the Mahatma: Bishop V. S. Azariah and the Travails of Christianity in British India* (Grand Rapids: Eerdmans, 2000), p. 326.

ary, J. W. Pickett, was strangely silent. When McGavran eventually issued a humiliating apology it concealed his private belief that Gandhi had actually made the threats regarding state action against conversion. Until his death in 1990 McGavran insisted privately that he had told the truth about this encounter. Azariah and Gandhi had lied.[2]

Azariah's biographer sides with McGavran about what really happened in that meeting between Gandhi and his arch enemy Azariah behind closed doors. She has good reason to do so. Gandhi spoke openly and often on the subject of conversion, but always in a critical way. In his collected reflections he expresses his dislike of Christian conversion.[3] He had reportedly made statements earlier in the decade that he would use the law to stop Christian conversions from happening were it in his power. Whether McGavran got the details correct in his article may never be known with any certainty. Whether Gandhi was against Christian conversion in general and the mass conversion of his beloved Dalit during the Dornakal revival in particular is a matter of public record.

WHAT ABOUT CONVERSION?

What is the role of conversion in global revivals? After the storms of volatility have broken, after the new leaders with their new light have emerged, then comes the people movement. This movement of people happens through conversion, something most of us know a great deal about but about which great mystery and controversy remain.

The McGavran episode reminds me how central and controversial is the role of the conversion in global revivals. I want to revisit the Dornakal revival of the 1920s and 1930s and the conversion controversy that it inspired. Though Gandhi disliked Christian conversion one aspect of his critique was either missed or marginalized by his Christian opponents—the role of new wineskins, new forms of Christian com-

---

[2]Ibid., p. 327.
[3]Cf. Mahatma Gandhi, *All Men Are Brothers: Autobiographical Reflections* (London: Continuum, 1980).

munity, in conversion. Here's my hunch: by downplaying the need for more indigenous forms of Christian community, the Dornakal revival under Azariah weakened the quality of and complicated the conflict over Christian conversion—a conflict that continues today. What follows is the story of the Dalit revival in Dornakal through the eyes of the main actors in the conversion drama of 1938.

BACKGROUND TO THE DORNAKAL REVIVAL

Let me start my story with a confession. I had my own mental picture of Dalits. I pictured the typical Dalit as a beggar in a loin cloth sitting in a gutter along a busy street in a crowded Indian city. What I wasn't expecting was Anderson.

When Lois and I spent a year studying global revivals in Edinburgh one of the first people we met was Anderson. He was an ordained Anglican minister in the Church of South India. He was articulate and educated, recently accepted for doctoral studies at the university. He led our little campus Bible study at New College. We engaged in great debates about Pentecostalism and revivalism and justice issues. We went to movies and enjoyed the occasional meal together at the local Nepalese restaurant on Leith Walk. He remains a great friend. He also remains a Dalit.

Representing almost 20 percent of India's billion people, Dalits defy stereotypes. Yet Anderson came to Edinburgh to work on a liberation theology that would address the endemic poverty, deprivation, landlessness and exploitation that is the Dalit experience. Anderson reminds me that Christianity not only has a long and important history in India but also that the church requires periodic moments of renewal, such as the Dornakal revival, to awaken from its institutional slumbers and restore the spiritual and material lives of the "wretched of the earth."

Neglect of the poor by the church was not always the case. The stories of the apostle Thomas preaching freedom in Christ to first-century Hindus in southern India is an unquestioned fact for the majority of Indian Christians that come under the wide and multifaceted umbrella of Malabar Christianity. Roman Catholicism arrived with Portuguese traders in the sixteenth century. Justice was not always served by the colonial forms of Christianity that came with them. Powerful Jesuits like Francis Xavier and Robert De Nobili sought to soften the blow of Catholic colonialism by developing more indigenously sensitive ministries to low-caste fisherman and high-caste Brahmins respectively.

Protestantism got a late start but had its champions from the late eighteenth century onward with pietists like Bartholomew Ziegenbalg, Baptists like William Carey, and, in the early part of the nineteenth century, Presbyterians like Alexander Duff. Education and Bible translation helped to soften the blow of British imperialism, but Christianity nonetheless struggled to be seen as something more than the religious arm of colonialism. By 1900 Anglicanism, favored church of the colonial power, was established widely over the subcontinent. Yet its impact on poverty and injustice as well as its translation of the message into indigenous forms was minimal. All of that would change dramatically through a young Indian Anglican convert named V. S. Azariah.

THE BISHOP

Vedanayakam S. Azariah was born in 1874 in South India, in the Tamil Nadir village of Vellalanvilai, Tinnevelly district. His father, Thomas, was an Anglican priest, having become a Christian in 1839 under the influence of the legendary Welsh missionary, John Thomas. Azariah's two half brothers by his father's first wife pursued distinguished academic careers as scholars of Sanskrit, the sacred language of Hinduism.

The young Azariah attended Madras Christian College (1896) but failed to gain his degree due to an illness. There he encountered a popular missionary strategy that he was later to reject. The principal of the college, William Miller (1862-1907), was the leading exponent of the strategy by which high-caste Hindus would undergo a transformation of their worldview through liberal arts education even without a presentation of the gospel. The aim, as the prospectus of the college stated, was "simply to convey through the channel of a good education as great an amount of truth as possible to the native mind, especially of Bible truth." As truth gradually penetrated the Hindu mind it would change the "thoughts and values of the entire culture." This was a strategy which did not require conversion in any conventional sense, so gradual would be the change. Though Azariah would reject the strategy as too indirect, he nonetheless imbibed some of its values for he left Madras Christian College deeply convinced that Western culture contained many strengths needed by India.[4]

Azariah worked with the YMCA from 1895 (while still a student) until 1909. His international trips as a YMCA representative and evangelist enlarged his world and deepened his commitment to ecumenical Christianity. His friendship with John R. Mott enabled him to attend a number of conferences that further expanded his horizons. From 1909 until 1912 he was an independent missionary working out of an indigenous agency he helped to found. It was in this capacity that he attended Edinburgh's World Missionary Conference in 1910 and issued his famous call for the Western church not to send missionaries but "to give us friends." Azariah's cry of the heart came from a deeper vision of social, economic and racial reconciliation in Christ, a vision that would inspire much of his evangelism and ministry later as a bishop.

It was during his years as a YMCA evangelist that he developed the new light message that would have such an impact on the Dalit communities of Dornakal. The influence of American evangelical missionary George Sherwood Eddy (1871-1963) was immense. They shared a deep belief in the power of revival to expand and transform the church. In 1899 they collaborated on a biography of Charles Grandison Finney, "the father of revivalism" in America. Azariah translated Finney's *Lectures on Revival* into Tamil. In his book *Pathfinders of the World Missionary Crusade* (1945), Eddy recalled the vision that he shared with Azariah. "Our objective was both individual and social," he later wrote.

---

[4]Harper, *Shadow of the Mahatma*, p. 148.

They would "work with all Christian forces as one team" in order to "raise up Indian leaders for the Christianization of their own land." Once this was accomplished, these leaders would "change the whole social order, building a new India as part of a new world."

The two friends and colleagues later disagreed over how best to apply the gospel to social issues. Eddy was a pacifist and strong supporter of the Christian socialism personified by Ramsay MacDonald and the British Labour Party. Azariah was also committed to the social application of the gospel but disliked aligning the gospel with any particular political ideology or party. Both took seriously the YMCA ideal of spiritual, physical, intellectual and social development. But each understood in different ways how "India's social regeneration would be brought about by Christian evangelization."[5]

AZARIAH ON EVANGELICAL CONVERSION

In 1912 Azariah became India's first Anglican bishop in the newly created diocese of Dornakal in what is now Andhra Pradesh. Always an evangelist at heart, Azariah initiated an aggressive preaching program in the Dalit villages of his diocese. The results were immediate. Susan Harper writes that between 1921 and 1931 "conversions to Christianity occurred in Andhra at a faster rate than" anywhere else in South Asia. Over twelve thousand new converts joined the church each month for a decade. The overall growth rate of Indian Protestant Christianity (along with Burma) for this key decade was 41 percent. The great majority of these new converts were Dalit. Azariah gained international fame in Christian circles for his successful leadership.

These mass movements of Dalit converts (primarily among the Mala and Madiga tribes) is an expression of a global revival. The social, economic and cultural volatility of colonialism coupled with new nationalist movements created the matrix for renewal. New light leaders like Azariah with their progressive evangelicalism provided the new para-

---

[5]Ibid., p. 59.

digm of healing and hope. The new paradigm was explosive and ignited one of the largest revivals in the twentieth century with almost a million converts stretched over a ten-year period.

After the Dornakal revival began the questions about conversion multiplied. Some questions were raised by the missionary advocates of revival. Donald McGavran and his mentor J. Wascom Pickett were both evangelicals who nevertheless felt that the key to conversions lay in appealing to the converts longing for social and economic uplift. The facts of the gospel would be declared, of course, but the emphasis would be on benefits to be gained by becoming a Christian. Azariah agreed with this approach to a degree but was reluctant to reduce conversion to vitalistic factors such as social uplift. Though he supported Pickett's study of the mass movements of India, he stressed the role of revivalistic elements of the primal Christian past such as the work of the Holy Spirit even more than the missionaries did. As Azariah said in the preface to Pickett's 1938 follow-up study to the mass movements, "The forces that make for change of religious allegiance on the part of men are many and often beyond human analysis."[6]

Other questions were raised by the missionary critics of mass conversions. If I convert to Christianity simply because my extended family does, how sincere or deep is my conversion?

To answer the "quality" question some background might be in order. Dalit mass movements into Christianity had begun in the nineteenth century. The pattern, though with local variety, seemed fairly clear. First is the rise of the Dalit leader with a vision of the Christian message that appeals to the masses. Next comes the communication of the new message to family networks and neighbors. Third is the involvement by the missionary who sees something happening and seeks to give encouragement. During stage three when the evangelistic outreach intensified, Dalit converts came in large numbers. Historian John Webster disputes Pickett's definition of a mass movement as one "char-

---

[6]J. Waskom Pickett, *Christ's Way to India's Heart* (London: United Society of Christian Literature, 1938), p. 6.

acterized by group decision."[7] He insists on the role of the individual in responding to both the message and the social network in making a decision.[8] Conversion does not have to be either individual or group. It can be, and in the majority world often is, a matter of both. After the stage of conversion comes the deepening of faith and commitment. This fourth and final stage was the saturation stage. This meant the struggle, often without much success, to instruct and baptize those seeking conversion. Often the evangelists regrouped, trained others and continued the movement for several decades.

Historian Chandra Mallampalli supports Webster. He describes what a typical Dalit convert might experience in the midst of a million-person movement such as the Dornakal revival. Along with the call to accept Christ was a call to certain acts of commitment that would have deepened and cemented the decision in individual lives. Many of these acts of commitment involved giving up practices offensive to higher-caste Hindus:

> Converts also abandoned their caste names for new Christian ones, which were often taken from the Bible. Removal of the juttu (the tuft of hair, signifying Hindu identity) from male converts and traditional caste markings from women became important means of demarcating the new Christian identity. . . . The movement against the consumption of carrion among Madiga leather workers was a crucial reform for ridding them of their stigma of impurity. The diocese also prohibited converts from participating in any form of idol worship or festivals associated with Hindu sacrifices, rituals or ceremonies.[9]

Other questions about Dalit conversion came from Gandhi and the Hindu nationalists. Would not these mass movements of the Dalit out of Hinduism and into a foreign religion weaken the campaign for independence? Azariah rejected this objection. Christian conversion would not

[7]John C. Webster, *The Dalit Christians: A History* (Delhi: ISPCK, 1992), p. 58.
[8]Ibid.
[9]Chandra Mallampalli, *Christians and Public Life in Colonial South India, 1863-1937: Contending with Marginality* (London: Rutledge Curzon, 2004), p. 187.

undermine Indian patriotism and nationalism. In a letter written in the 1930s and later published in 1945, Azariah wrote, "My love to my countrymen and my nationalism—they think—ought to be measured by my attitude to Congress [Gandhi's party] or to political problems. . . . If I labour to remove illiteracy, dirt, social enslavement and superstition of the neglected and the unprivileged or underprivileged—am I to be reckoned a foreigner with foreign sympathies with no love for my country?" He went on to argue that wearing a particular kind of dress or not eating in a certain way does not mean one is un-Indian or unpatriotic.[10]

Azariah's view of Dalit conversion was an attempt to balance various elements. He defended the Dalit motivation of social uplift. He subscribed to the Eddy vision of a new India and a new world transformed by the gospel. He also felt that conversion was compatible with nationalism and "Indian-ness." Yet his concept of nationalism was more Western than Gandhian. In the last analysis Azariah is an Anglican evangelical. He has more in common with a William Wilberforce than a Mahatma Gandhi. For Azariah changing the nation meant changing the heart. Thus the most important aspects of conversion were those elements found in communion, "the cross and resurrection." His vision of the church was a mildly indigenized nineteenth-century evangelical Anglicanism. More radical expressions of Christian community were not entertained.

Azariah's role as the new light leader of the Dornakal revival and defender of its model of conversion makes him the central figure in the drama of Dalit mass movements into Christianity. But his views on revival and conversions were not the only ones. There were also the missionaries.

THE MISSIONARIES ON PRAGMATIC CONVERSION

The missionaries involved in the 1938 conversion crisis, J. W. Pickett and Donald McGavran, shared many things in common with Azariah

---

[10]Harper, *Shadow of the Mahatma*, p. 337.

on the subject of conversion. J. W. Pickett expressed his views on the subject with great clarity in the two major studies for which he is remembered. His 1933 study grew out of a directive from the National Christian Council of India, Burma and Ceylon meeting in Madras in 1928 to study these mass movements. The council chairman, Bishop Azariah, with the encouragement of Christian statesman John R. Mott, assembled the research team with Pickett as director of the survey. The purpose of the survey was "for the first time" to "assemble and compare information regarding chief types of the mass movement in different regions which should be invaluable to leaders of the Indian church, and of the missionary organizations co-operating therewith."[11]

On almost every page in Pickett's study of the Dalit revival is the social and economic benefit of Christian conversion. One of the most powerful effects of Christianity on the Dalit convert was in the area of alleviating the feeling of inferiority. In light of the Christian gospel and Christian worship the "old inhibitions are broken and unsuspected powers are released." Pickett noted the importance of training and school for new converts and their families but admitted that there was a shortage of schools in general and of good schools in particular. In his opinion this was a crucial area of need not so much for the local church but for the mission agency in order "to fight illiteracy, oppression, and poverty." This need "has lost none of its urgency."[12]

Pickett defended his "conversion as uplift" model by noting how Hindu neighbors responded to Dalits who became Christian. He admitted that there were a few Hindus who exhibited "unreasoning hostility" to Christian converts, but they were the exception. The majority of those interviewed were "appreciative of the character of the Christians, and of the influence of Christianity." Behavior changes like giving up scavenging, working harder, not drinking or gambling, and not practicing sorcery most impressed their non-Christian neighbors.[13]

---

[11]J. Waskom Pickett, *Christian Mass Movements in India* (New York: Abingdon, 1933), p. 12.
[12]Ibid.
[13]Ibid., p. 209.

In his final study of Dalit conversion, Pickett continued to strike a pragmatic chord. In *Christ's Way to India's Heart,* Pickett gave fourteen conclusions to his study of the mass movements in Andhra Desa since 1933. Two stand out as particularly telling of his position. One concerns the "menace of caste." He insisted that everything must be done to produce churches that cross this divide. A second conclusion was the "handicap of foreignness." Pickett cannot escape the conviction that the "growth of the church is retarded by the aspect of foreignness and promoted by evidence of being Indian and indigenous." One way to compensate for the foreignness, which the missionaries were ill-equipped to address, was to increase the preaching of social and economic uplift. Pickett stressed how Dalit conversion improved the economic condition of those surveyed. He seemed almost defensive about the social and economic benefit of conversion: "the Church has no reason to apologize if its ministry to the poor reduces hunger and disease among them."[14]

Donald McGavran followed his mentor in stressing the "this worldly" benefits of conversion. Doctrinal and biblical content was important but it took a back seat. McGavran rejected the term "revival" to describe the Dalit mass movements because of its American connotations as "church growth from among a discipled people or nation" or even worse, local church renewal without any numeric growth. "When we speak here of 'Church growth,'" wrote McGavran in 1937, ". . . we do not mean the spiritual or intellectual advance of existing members of static central stations churches." McGavran was concerned only with expansion. Expansion meant numbers and converts. McGavran's conclusion from Pickett's study was that growth must take place in what he would later call a "people group" (originally defined in terms of jati or endogamous group created by the caste). One must accept the limits of culture and caste so that people may come to Christ with others on their social stratum. Such movements should begin not with missionaries but with converted

---

[14]Pickett, *Christ's Way to India's Heart,* p. 129.

leaders from the social group. These insights, gleaned from Pickett, would become the basis of his influential theories of church growth that have had such an impact in North America.[15]

For the missionaries, conversion meant preaching Christ, but preaching him pragmatically. The gospel is a force for progress. The revivalistic element, returning to the primal community of Acts meant more for Azariah than for Pickett and McGavran though the revivalistic note is not absent. The heritage of William Miller and Alexander Duff (teaching the superiority of Western culture as a preparation for the gospel) resurfaced in Pickett and McGavran in a new way. The new missionaries were preaching for conversion but it was a gospel of better living through evangelical Christianity. Christianity commended itself to the Dalit for its social and economic value. It was the path to eternal life but that path must be built with the bricks of progress and economic uplift.

THE DALIT MODEL OF POLITICAL CONVERSION

Conversion meant certain things to Bishop Azariah and slightly different things to the missionaries. But what did it mean to Dalit Hindus who watched from the sideline while their sisters and brothers walked the sawdust trail of Christian conversion? There is no better person to ask than Bhimrao Ramji Ambedkar (1891-1956). Ambedkar was born into a Dalit family in western India. The humiliation suffered at the hands of upper-caste fellow students during his early education left a permanent scar. After higher education in the United Stated, Britain and Germany he returned to India. After an unpleasant experience in the caste-conscious Indian public service, he entered law and soon found himself in politics as the spokesman for the Dalit of India. In a nation in which religion was a major force in public life, Ambedkar was willing to play the "conversion card" for the sake of his constituents.

---

[15]Donald McGavran, "When the Church Grows," in *Church Growth and Group Conversion* (Pasadena, Calif.: William Carey Press, 1937), p. 4.

Azariah's leadership of the movement among Malas and Madigas in the diocese of Dornakal in the 1920s and 1930s gained national attention. Ambedkar was convinced that he could marshal this history into political leverage.

His initial foray into national politics put him into conflict with Gandhi. In 1932 the British government granted the "communal award" which gave voting rights to various "special electorates." Ambedkar had lobbied for the Dalit to be included in the communal award. In this he was successful. Gandhi, however, opposed separating his beloved Harijan (children of God, Gandhi's name for the Dalit) from the Hindu majority. Imprisoned at the time, Gandhi went on a "fast to the death" which eventually forced a compromise with Ambedkar. The Poona Pact of 1932 between Hindu nationalist leaders including Ambedkar gave up the idea of separate electorates but granted the Dalit community increased representation for a ten-year period. Ambedkar's frustration with Gandhi and Hindu nationalism grew.

When the controversy of 1938 erupted, Ambedkar was active behind the scenes. He had "regular contact" with Pickett and helped persuade the latter not to trust Gandhi. Pickett recorded Ambedkar's influence on his thinking in a letter of the previous year. Regarding Gandhi's increasing hostile statements about Christianity, conversion and missionaries in the mid-1930s, Pickett wrote, "I discussed this matter last week with Dr. Ambedkar." Pickett was convinced by the Dalit leader that "Hindus under the leadership of Gandhi are likely to make a sustained effort to legislate for the control of conversion."[16]

Ambedkar eventually converted to Buddhism in 1956 bringing several hundred thousand Dalit with him in one of the largest mass movements of conversion in Indian history. The Dalit leader was a political pragmatist on conversion. All that mattered in conversion was removal of the hated curse of Hindu caste consciousness. He had little interest in the revivalistic elements of conversion—the return to a primal or

---

[16]Harper, *Shadow of Mahatma*, p. 330.

ideal past, an element so central to Azariah and assumed as necessary by the missionaries. On the subject of conversion Ambedkar, therefore, was probably closer to the missionary position than was Azariah who balanced social uplift, "Indianness" and revivalism more evenly. He was most at odds with the central figure of the 1938 conversion conflict—Mahatma Gandhi.

THE MAHATMA AND THE CONVERSION OF THE CHURCH

How did Gandhi see the conflict with Bishop Azariah? Born in Porbandar in 1869, five years before Azariah's birth, Gandhi received his early education in India. Eventually he traveled to London for his law degree. After completing his studies he spent twenty-one years as a lawyer in South Africa before returning to his native India in 1915, just three years after Azariah had become India's first Anglican bishop. As Harper writes, it was Gandhi rather than Azariah who was in various ways the "foreigner in his own land."[17] When in the 1930s the British government expanded the electoral rights of more Indian groups based on "religious, caste and economic status," both Gandhi and Azariah objected. Gandhi wanted the Dalit to be kept within Hinduism while Azariah feared marginalizing Christians by making them an electoral category. Both clashed with Ambedkar. In 1936 and 1937 Gandhi became more critical of mass conversions feeling that they threatened the nationalist cause. While admitting conversion may have done the Dalit some economic or social good it was still "a distasteful part" of the progress of his Harijans.[18]

Gandhi believed in conversion but a different kind of conversion. He believed in conversion to his philosophy of *satyagraha*. Gandhi entered the debates of the 1930s with a prior commitment to a philosophy of nation building to which he sought to make converts. Called "Truth force" or "Soul force," *satyagraha* was "an unending, relentless, dialecti-

---

[17]Ibid.
[18]Ibid., p. 322.

81

cal quest for truth." Gandhi claimed that "it is to violence, and therefore, to all tyranny, all injustice, what light is to darkness." Its purpose he declared was "conversion and never coercion" to an ongoing, neverending search for truth.[19]

For Gandhi the main roadblock to realizing his national dream was not the intransigence of the British but the missionary activity of the church. Gandhi appreciated Christ but hated the church. He not only disliked its corruptions, he was revolted by its existence. The very concept of the church was not only foreign to his Hinduism but a rival to his nationalism. "I consider Western Christianity in its practical working," he wrote, "a negation of Christ's Christianity." Gandhi confessed that he could not "conceive Jesus, if he was living in the flesh in our midst, approving of modern Christian organizations, public worship, or modern ministry."[20]

Conversion which led to church membership was for Gandhi both the destruction of a culture and a threat to nationalism. He approved only of missionaries who practiced humanitarian service "without the ulterior motive of converting India, or at least her unsophisticated villagers, to Christianity and destroying their social superstructure which notwithstanding its many defects has withstood from time immemorial the onslaughts on it from within and from without." This is a strong statement of the primacy of culture over everything else. Hinduism is true because it is "our" religion. Christianity was for Gandhi both a rival religion and foreign culture despite its long history in India.

Gandhi's "nativism" (what anthropologists call a commitment to local tradition and the immediate past coupled with a suspicion of anything foreign) was instructive, however. He saw something that many of the other parties in the conflict of 1938 did not see as clearly. His critique of Dalit conversion concerned not only the departure from Hindu culture but entrance into a foreign structure—the church. Mass

---

[19]Glyn Richards, *The Philosophy of Gandhi* (London: Curzon Press, 1982), pp. 50-55.
[20]Ainslie T. Embree, *Utopias in Conflict: Religion and Nationalism in Modern India* (Berkeley: University of California Press, 1990), p. 45.

movements into colonial church structures simply would not do. Though Dalit leaders, missionaries and Indian bishops might talk about Christian conversion in evangelical or economic terms, Gandhi, the nationalist, seemed to see conversion as too closely associated with a larger and more threatening whole (the British Empire and Western culture). The Dornakal revival in the 1920s thus sparked a major debate about conversion that divided Indian Christian leaders, foreign missionaries, Dalit leaders and nationalist champions. Who was right?

CHRISTIAN CONVERSION AS A FOURFOLD REALITY

The Dornakal revival of the 1920s and 1930s is an example of a global revival. Dalits were prepared for the revival during a problem stage in which a volatile India made their precarious status politically and economically even more uncertain. The arrival of Azariah, the bishop evangelist, in Dornakal in 1912 paved the way for phase two. As a new light leader, Azariah proclaimed an evangelical social gospel that combined personal and social liberation through faith in Christ. Through mass conversions the revival became a matter of national interest eventually attracting the attention of Gandhi. The final phase of the revival saw continuing church growth and rising conflict with Hindu nationalism. The conversion crisis of 1938 brought this growing conflict into sharp focus. I conclude the story of the Dornakal revival by analyzing the role of conversion in Christian renewal movements.

While "outsider" descriptions of Christian conversion, such as one finds in the social sciences, can provide insight, I believe that "insider" descriptions of conversion are more helpful to understand its nature and role in global revivals. For this we need to look at the theological dynamics of global revivals and the light they shed on the drama of conversion that lies at their center. I can think of no better place to begin than in Luke's description of mass conversion in Jerusalem in the first global revival of Christian history.[21]

---

[21]A valuable study of conversion from the perspective of the social sciences is Lewis R. Rambo,

CONVERSION IN ACTS 2: BEHOLDING, BELIEVING, BELONGING, BEHAVING

On the day of Pentecost three thousand people responded to Peter's message that the death and resurrection of Jesus had inaugurated the new age of the kingdom of God, were filled with the Holy Spirit, had their sins forgiven, joined the new church of Jerusalem and began living missional lives that involved the community of goods. All this is described by Luke, the father not only of Christian history but also of global revival history as well.

In Luke's account, conversion plays a central role. Let me offer a working definition of the kind of conversion one sees in Acts 2 and indeed throughout the book. Christian conversion, for Luke, is a turning away of the whole person from an old reality in which Christ is marginal to a new reality in which Christ is central. This reorientation of one's whole life has a beginning but, as Andrew Wall pointed out, should probably never have an end. This initial and ongoing conversion involves change in several key relationships, which taken together give to us a rounded portrait of Christian conversion which would be recognized by an insider in a Christian revival. Four of those key changes (or turns) are: (1) a new vision of the future (beholding), (2) a new sense of personal liberation (believing), (3) a new community (belonging) and (4) a new mission in life (behaving).

The first element in a Christian conversion according to Luke is beholding, or seeing Christ as the key to history. Acts 2 is dominated not by the descent of the Spirit, which is mentioned briefly, nor by the inward response of the crowd, but by the message of Peter (2:14-40) with its focus on the remarkable life and achievements of Jesus the Messiah.

Peter's first concern was not an emotional response of the audience

Understanding Religious Conversion (New Haven, Conn.: Yale University Press, 1993). See also the fine historical study of evangelical conversions by D. Bruce Hindmarsh, *The Evangelical Conversion Narrative: Spiritual Autobiography in Early Modern England* (New York: Oxford University Press, 2005), which concludes with a sample of non-Western conversion narratives.

to his appeal, but a cognition of the centrality of Jesus Christ to history. His message is about how the death and resurrection of Christ fulfills Old Testament prophecy about the future, the age to come that brings to and end the present evil age. Peter reaches his climax of this new vision of the future in verse 36: "Therefore let all Israel be assured of this: God has made this Jesus, whom you crucified, both Lord and Christ." Peter's first concern is that people see something, not necessarily feel something. They need to see that Jesus has turned the old view of history into a new view, with him at the center. Conversion begins with beholding.

The next two elements in the mass conversions at Pentecost involved audience response in the form of inner conviction (believing) and baptism by the Spirit and by water (belonging). In verse 37 Luke tells us that the audience "were cut to the heart and said to Peter and the other apostles, 'Brothers, what shall we do?'" Peter's answer? "Repent and be baptized, every one of you, in the name of Jesus Christ for the forgiveness of your sins. And you will receive the gift of the Holy Spirit." Repentance is a restatement of his call in verse 21: "Everyone who calls on the name of the Lord shall be saved." Those who turn from their previous worldview (in which Christ was marginal) to a worldview in which he is central (Lord) have moved from beholding to believing. This belief in Christ and his benefits produces a powerful sense of personal liberation because in this new age of history sins are forgiven and peace with God as much loved sons and daughters becomes our new identity.

Baptism reminds us that conversion involves more than beholding and believing. It also involves belonging or new affiliation. We join this radical community of those who have also seen the centrality of Christ and experienced his personal liberating power. Luke is careful to note that "Those who accepted his message were baptized, and about three thousand were added to their number that day" (Acts 2:41).

The fourth element of conversion is behaving. "By their fruit you will recognize them," Jesus once said (Mt 7:16). No conversion is complete without mission. Later in Acts, Luke will present the conversion of Paul (three times actually). Some have questioned whether the account of Paul on the Damascus road is about conversion at all, so strongly does the element of calling to mission play in the narrative. But Luke would not permit such a distinction. True conversion always involves the call to mission. The concept of a Christian without a call is not part of Luke's mental world. In Acts 2:44-47 and following Luke gave one of the most haunting description s of a revival fellowship in all of Christian history: "All the believers were together and had everything in common. Selling their possessions and goods, they gave to anyone as he had need. Every day they continued to meet together in the temple courts. They broke bread in their homes and ate together with glad and sincere hearts." Not only is this a description of radical community at work it is more pointedly a picture of the missional lifestyle of the mass converts.

Jonathan Edwards identified the twelfth and most visible of the distinguishing marks of a true work of the Spirit of God as the missional lifestyle motivated by radical love. This was for Edwards the sign of signs in his *Religious Affections*. His later call for concerts of prayer for the beginning of a global Protestant mission as part of his postmillennial theology of world transformation through the gospel was a commitment to this fourth element of conversion. The Puritans called it new obedience. Edwards simply called it love.

What about the role of the Holy Spirit in conversion? What role does he play in the conversion quartet of beholding, believing, belonging and behaving? For Luke the Spirit is central. The Spirit is involved in the initial conversion stages of beholding and believing. He is also involved in the more ongoing aspects of conversion of belonging and behaving.

This missional lifestyle is seen only periodically in the history of Christianity and typically during times of revival—monasticism in the early and medieval church on all the continents, evangelical revivals in the north Atlantic community in the eighteenth centuries climaxing with the antislavery campaign in England under Clarkson and Wilberforce, and global revivals in the twentieth century with their new sense of reverse mission as they seek to reclaim Europe and America for the gospel.

Many of the most successful revival movements in modern history have created new structures to contain the converts of their movements. Methodism for decades remained within the Anglican Church but held their special "classes" and "bands" as part of a more revolutionary fellowship that made up a "church within a church." After the death of Wesley the new renewal structure became a new denomination. In the East Africa revival most of the fruits of new conversion were contained in the historic churches of Uganda and Kenya by the Revival Brethren with their house groups, prayer meetings and annual conferences. Similarly the enormous charismatic renewal within mainline churches around the world and within Roman Catholicism has taken place through charismatic renewal fellowships where local expression to the broader charismatic movement is shaped and expressed. Luke's perspective in Acts 2 may be telling. After Peter's successful new light message three thousand people responded in a mass conversion that initiated Christianity's first revival movement.

Luke's concern is less with the character of individual conversions and more with the creation of a radical community. He ends his account of Pentecost with a portrait of a new community. Luke indicates that there were traditional as well as novel elements in this new community. It was a deeply Jewish community in that its central focus was a return to the sacred promise of messianic expectation and fulfillment which Peter persuaded them had occurred in Jesus Christ crucified and risen. It was a radical community in that they broke with tradition by practicing the "community of goods" which made sure that material and economic needs were taken care of in the name of their new messiah. It was also traditional to the degree that they fit into the urban pattern of a Jerusalem Jew with regular visits to the temple punctuated with private fellowship around the table. The reaction of the surrounding community at least initially was positive, says Luke, for the new church enjoyed "the favor of all the people" (Acts 2:47). It is an ideal to which subsequent church movements have aspired with periodic success.

OF NEW WINE AND OLD WINESKINS: CONVERSION AS BELONGING TO A FOREIGN STRUCTURE

It may seem a long way from Jerusalem to Delhi. Nonetheless the Acts 2 model sheds light on the conversion crisis of 1938. I may sympathize with Azariah and the missionaries. I may understand why Ambedkar would use conversion as a tool of economic liberation and political power. I may ardently oppose Gandhi and his position that conversion should be banned by law. But it is to Gandhi that I will give the last word in this debate about conversion because he saw something that the Bishop, the missionaries and the Dalit elite either overlooked or underemphasized. Gandhi, more than any of the main parties in the debate about conversion, saw the central role of belonging.

The revivals in Korea and Nigeria that we have looked at so far underscore the same point. The Korean church by 1907 was seen increasingly as an indigenous structure even though it bore Western denominational names. Revival had changed the old wineskins into new ones. The Babalola revival of Nigeria broke out of the Anglican Church because it was unwilling to contain the new light offered by charismatic and restorationist forms of the faith. Conversion was often out of Anglicanism and into the new wineskins of radical community provided by the Aladura churches. In our next chapter we will see how the East Africa revival made the belonging issue central and sought to change the Anglican church of Uganda to conform to the demands of global revival.

The clash over conversion in 1938 was but one episode in an ongoing conflict that continues today. In 1998 after attacks on tribal Christians in Gujarat, the Bharatiya Janata Party's (BJP) Atal Bihari Vajpayee, the prime minister of India, refused to respond to Christian requests for action and instead called for "national debate on conversions." He justified his call as "something consistent with the outlook of the Mahatma."

If Vajpayee's claim was true then his protest against Christian or Buddhist conversions out of Hinduism had less to do with issues of beholding, believing or even behaving. The great stumbling block was belonging. When the convert affiliates with a religious structure that seems opposed to the national life and culture it arouses the kind of conflict that occurred in the India of 1938 and 1998.[22]

By looking at Dalit mass movements in the 1920s and 1930s as revivals we can see this important fourth dimension to Christian conversion. Conversion is not just to God or to the future but also to a visible community. Caught in the middle of a tense struggle between rival Hindu nationalist leaders like Gandhi and Ambedkar, Azariah, though longing for an end to caste consciousness, called Dalits to a conversion of beholding and believing without offering an indigenous church where new kinds of belonging could take place. The new wine of beholding and believing required appropriate wineskins where belonging could happen. The church of the colonial elite was not the right kind of wineskin. Pickett and McGavran crafted a model of conversion that stressed the material benefits more than beholding or believing. They realized that conversion could be stalled by the problem of the church's "foreignness." But the only solution they could think of was to increase stress on how horrible Dalit lives were under Hinduism and how improved they would be under Christianity.

Though Gandhi hated conversion the most, he seemed to realize the importance of the belonging component better than the others in the debate. They sought to sidestep the problem of the church. Gandhi, almost alone, demanded that this problem be addressed. The need to indigenize the church was noted by most but nothing was done about it. Imagine the apostles telling the three thousand converts of Acts 2 to meet at the local imperial temple where pigs would be offered to the

[22]Mallampalli, *Christians and Public Life*, p. 5. For additional background and a larger view of the conversion conflict in modern India see also Chandra Mallampalli, "South Asia, 1911-2003," in *The Cambridge History of Christianity: World Christianities c.1914-c.2000*, ed. Hugh McCleod (Cambridge: Cambridge University Press, 2006).

emperor. Despite quality believing, beholding and behaving, the Christian movement would have failed from the outset.

Luke made sure to end his account of mass conversion in Acts 2 by showing a radical community that combined both traditional and innovative elements but one that elicited general approval from the locals, was grounded in their cultural past and would not be confused as a symbol of colonial power. Gandhi consistently pointed to this same element of belonging as the missing piece in the mass conversions in Dornakal. Gandhi instinctively knew what Luke realized so well: no conversion is complete without the conversion of the church.

5

NOTHING BUT THE BLOOD

William Nagenda and the
East African Revival in Uganda

The East Africa revival changed my life. In 1977 this movement, famous around the world, confronted me in the person of Kefa Sempangi. Kefa and his wife Peninah were Ugandan exiles from Amin's Uganda and studying at Westminster seminary in Philadelphia. Kefa was not your typical theological student. He had a Ph.D. in art history, having studied under one of my intellectual heroes, Hans Rookmaaker, at the Free University of Amsterdam. Kefa was a lecturer in art history at Makerere University, one of Africa's most respected institutions of higher education. He was also the pastor of the fourteen-thousand-member Redeemed Church of Kampala. Coming from New England where Protestant churches tended to be small, I found the very existence of such a church almost a miracle.

Part of that miracle was the power of the East Africa revival that had touched his life as a young man of twenty in 1961. His friend Mondo had challenged him that churchgoing was not enough. He needed to learn to "walk in the light" by publicly confessing his sins to other believers. Reluctant at first, Kefa soon joined a revival fellowship and found that open confession led not to scandal or condemnation but to new acceptance and deeper worship. Kefa learned the power of the cross to cleanse and liberate. It was this power that enabled Kefa to pursue art history as well as to found the Redeemed Church.[1]

The larger reason Kefa had come to America after escaping Amin's reign of terror was to start the Africa Foundation, an organization to help Ugandan exiles around the world who had been forced to flee the madness of Idi Amin's rule. One of his projects was a pastoral training school for exiled Ugandans to be established in Kenya. He and his friends challenged my wife, Lois, and me to consider joining this project after I finished my doctoral studies. After agonizing weeks of prayer we heard God's voice calling us to join Kefa in this work. Though the pastoral training project was eventually dropped by Kefa's board, Lois and I were hooked. By 1980 my doctorate was done and we were on our way to Kenya to teach Christian history. Africa has been our principal place of service ever since.

Meeting Kefa and Peninah was my first exposure to the East Africa revival but not the last. During the last few decades in Africa I have learned much more about this remarkable movement.

One feature of it that has captured my attention was that it largely stayed inside the church. Many of the movements that have shaped the new world Christianity have led to the creation of new churches. This revival revitalized many of the "mainline Protestant" churches of East Africa in the years surrounding World War II. It is one thing to make a new church by separating from an old one. It is quite another to make an old church new again.

As I tell the story of the East Africa revival, I will give special attention to something mentioned in the previous chapter, the place of radical community in global revivals. What I hope to show is that the East Africa revival brought not one but several kinds of radical community to Ugandan Anglicanism and other historic mission churches in East Africa through an emphasis on personal holiness and biblical mission. The great difference within the movement and the kinds of radical

---

[1]F. Kefa Sempangi, *A Distant Grief: The Real Story Behind the Martyrdom of Christians in Uganda* (Glendale, Calif.: Regal, 1979).

community it created lay between *those who saw holiness as a means to mission* and *those who saw holiness as an end in itself.* Let me show you what I mean.

LOOKING FOR A HOLY GOD: THE STORY OF THE REVIVAL

The revival that so changed the life of Kefa and Peninah and tens of thousands of other East Africans had revolutionary beginnings—two revolutions, to be specific. During the late nineteenth century the kingdom of Buganda crashed head on with the outside world.

The first revolution that resulted was about power. The "oligarchical revolution" saw political power move from king to younger chiefs more open to foreign influence, from traditional kings to the younger nobility eager for education and mastery of the modern world. This power shift would have lasting repercussions for Ugandan society.

Second was the "Christian revolution" which shifted religious loyalties from Ganda traditional religion (*balubaale* deities that were linked to Lake Victoria and the sacred kings of Ganda tradition) to variant brands of Christianity. In the 1870s the Church Missionary Society sent the first wave of Protestant missionaries to Uganda after Henry Stanley published an appeal from the Kabaka Mutesa for Christian instruction. These Anglican evangelicals were led by a determined Scotsman, Alexander Mackay, who had left his engineering career to become a lay missionary. The team was soon challenged by equally talented Catholic missionaries in the form of the White Fathers.

After the death of the king of Buganda, Mutesa I, in 1884 and the ascension of his son, Mwanga, things turned bloody. The Ugandan Martyrs, as they are known to history, both Catholic and Protestant, paid for their faith with their lives. This bloody purge of Christians, like Amin's reign of terror in another generation, led to the king's downfall and the triumph of Protestant Christianity. Preaching and the political intervention by British Lord Lugard and his maxim gun sealed Mwanga's fate. A revival in the 1890s under George Pilkington, Bible translator and disciple maker, mobilized a new generation of evangelistic "readers" to spread the gospel throughout Buganda and the hinterlands by reading portions of vernacular Scripture. The results were spectacular. An Ugandan church of size and strength rose up in an African kingdom that was seen by many outside observers as a Muslim sea.

The first revolution led to British political linkage. The second revolution led to close association with "European missionaries." The Church Missionary Society, in particular, gained numerical dominance over Catholicism by the 1890s. The Church of Uganda emerged by 1900 as one of the central institutions of Gandan civilization.[2]

The Uganda Agreement of 1900 affected both revolutions. This agreement turned Buganda into a British protectorate with indirect rule through the Kabaka, regional chiefs and a representative assembly (*lukiko*). It also instituted hut taxes which promoted a cash economy. Other provisions permitted private ownership of land which encouraged the rise of a Gandan landed aristocracy who increasingly used members of other tribes as serfs to work their land. Tribal friction increased. Additionally the agreement of 1900 created a new Christendom in Uganda. Anglicanism became a de facto established church given its connection with the colonial power. Over time the passion of the revolutionary days soon faded. By the 1920s Ugandan culture "was the product of a rather unique alliance between British imperialists, British evangelicals, and Ganda aristocrats."[3]

The church paid heavily for this alliance. Movements of protest and renewal came like the long rains. The Society of the One Almighty God (KOAB) founded by Jesse Kate broke from the Church of Uganda around 1920. Kate's movement rejected the use of Western medicine and also protested the privileges which the agreement of 1900 had conferred upon the Bugandan elite. By 1921 the movement was in decline and its leaders in exile. A second protest movement erupted in 1929.

---

[2]Catherine Ellen Robins, "Tukutendereza: A Study of Social Change and Sectarian Withdrawal in the Balokole Revivan of Uganda" (Ph.D. diss., Columbia University, 1975), p. 71.
[3]Ibid., p. 87.

Reuben Spartas Mukasa rejected the white dominance in both church and state. His church, the African Orthodox Church, was an Ethiopian type AIC (African Initiated Church) calling for a shift in power and identity. The third movement belonged to a disaffected missionary, Mabel Ensor, who founded the Mengo Gospel Church in 1928 as a protest against "liberalism" within the Anglican Church.[4]

Conditions were ripe for revival. It was only a question of who and when. The main "who" came to the fore in 1929. Simeon Nsibambi, a member of the Ganda aristocracy, was a health officer in the colonial civil service whose quest for a deeper experience of God was the catalyst of the movement. Nsibambi's conversion was related to his envy over a friend who received a scholarship to study overseas after Nsibambi had been denied. His encounter with CMS missionary Joe Church in that same year led to a pivotal spiritual retreat of Bible study and prayer. This retreat triggered the creation of a vast network of Bible studies, prayer meetings, evangelistic missions and "deeper life" conferences that would span the ensuing decades. Nsibambi had "long been known as a dissenter" who had frequently complained to the bishop about problems in the church. After his personal renewal he stopped wearing Western style shoes and returned to the traditional Ganda thong sandal. He quit his job in the civil service and daily began to preach his message of awakening "in the streets, shops, hospitals . . . of Kampala."[5]

After meeting with Church, Nsibambi discipled a group of young men who spread the message of Christian renewal through deeper life teaching. One of the most dynamic of Nsibambi's early disciples was his own younger brother, Blasio Kigozi. Kigozi went with Joe Church to Gahini Hospital in Rwanda. There he proclaimed the new light message of the revival. Signs of new religious fervor at the hospital appeared in 1931 after the conversion of a coworker. Kigozi initiated early morning prayer meetings to pray for revival. Special "missions" to out-

---

[4]Ibid., p. 91.
[5]Ibid., p. 62.

lying areas now began. Soon the movement had acquired the pejorative term *abaka* (burning ones). By 1933 a large outdoor convention was held at Gahini with public preaching on sin, salvation and the importance of public confession. The revival entered a new phase after 1933. From a tiny cluster of disciples surrounding Nsibambi it had become a mass movement and was well on its way to becoming a global revival.

In 1934 Kigozi stepped out of the revival limelight to prepare for his ordination by the Church of Uganda. He returned to the movement a year later only to find a religious atmosphere approaching fever pitch: "Meetings for prayers and praise often went on for hours, right into the night, and sometimes right on to the early morning. . . . Voices were lost through much singing. . . . Men and women were saved, and children, sometimes crying out with tears at these gatherings."[6] By 1935 "signs were seen of a widespread movement."[7] Revival had broken out.

What was the message that captivated so many? No great miracles of healing marked what became known as the Balokole revival, as in the Babalola revival in Nigeria which was occurring roughly at the same time. There were no mass conversions on the scale of the Dornakal revival. Tongues played no role in the East Africa revival as it had with Pandita Ramabai's Bible women at Pune in India.

Perhaps the closest analogy is with Korea. Like the Korean revival of 1907, this was a movement that stressed existential liberation as a prerequisite for radical community and evangelical activism. At the heart of the revival was the power of public confession of sin and new cleansing from the gospel, cleansing that led to a life of holiness. There were a host of political, social and economic needs in the Uganda of the 1930s but what tens of thousands wanted most was the power to "walk in the light."

One reason for the priority of spiritual concerns was tradition. A new generation felt that they had betrayed their Christian ancestors of the 1890s who had paid for their faith with their lives. In contrast the

---

[6]Ibid., p. 136.
[7]Ibid., p. 137.

new generation was exploiting the faith of their fathers as a stepladder to academic scholarships, land acquisition and political influence. They were a "Judas" generation selling their Savior for silver. Furthermore they had betrayed not only their Christian ancestors but their God and his gospel. Waves of spiritual alienation swept over Nsibambi's generation. What gave the revival such relevance and power was the message that there was a way to restore the broken covenant with their martyred mothers and fathers and with the God who had so revolutionized their forebears. The new paradigm proclaimed by Nsibambi, Kigozi, Church and their associates was the power of the cross and the necessity of "walking in the light."

Kefa explained the appeal of the revival in these same terms. He described a typical conversion with his revival friend Mondo. "Everytime I met Mondo he would greet me with the threefold challenge: Are you repenting? Are you walking in the Light? Are you being broken?" To Kefa the significance of these questions was all too clear: "It was Mondo who taught me that walking in the light means a total sharing with my brother of my secrets. . . . 'When we share our secrets,' Mondo said, 'there is total identification with our brother. We have a reciprocal bond.'"[8] Walking in the light meant brokenness, in Luganda, *okumenyeka*. "To be broken," wrote Kefa, "is to have no pride, for where there is pride there is no confession and no forgiveness."[9] Walking in the light meant moving the double alienation that overshadowed most lives: distance from God and from one another. It broke down the barrier that prevented union, sonship and intimacy with God and one's fellow humanity. It meant the end of inner exile.

As appealing as the revival message was to its followers, many found the paradigm dangerous. To critics of the revival the movement was too negative and reactionary. Between 1935 and 1945 the Bugandan wing of the revival was essentially a protest against a dead church. In Robins's opinion "the religious revival which emerged in Buganda between

---

[8]Sempangi, *A Distant Grief,* p. 38.
[9]Ibid., p. 39.

1935 and 1940 was explicitly reformist in character, challenging clergy, African Christian leaders, and English missionaries to recognize 'coldness' and 'hidden sin' in the Ugandan church."[10] The revivalist's criticism of the church had wider implication, however. The call for change in the Church of Uganda was perceived by many as an attack on the social order as a whole, "undermining the basic values of the society."[11] The revivalists saw themselves as the "guardians of the authentic traditions of Ganda Protestantism, a faithful remnant in a nation of nominal Christians."[12] This spiritual elitism did not sit well with either the church establishment or societal leadership. The walls dividing revival and church were rising.

The critics admitted there were problems. It was clear to almost everyone that the power of the earlier Christian revolution had waned. In 1932 the bishop remarked that one of the earlier characteristics of the Ganda Christian movement, missionary commitment and service, was now "at a low ebb."[13] Several additional problems in the church were aired at the Synod of 1934. First was the return of polygyny. At a meeting attended by both clergy and chiefs several spoke up about the growing practice of Christian leaders taking extra wives. It was "difficult to find a chief who is living a strictly moral life" they complained.[14] Yet little to no discipline was practiced by the church. The second problem was the dwindling enthusiasm for full-time pastoral ministry. Recruits were hard to come by and the pay still abysmally low.[15] The clergy and the chiefs had little idea how to change things.

The revival leaders, on the other hand, were certain they had found the root problem. Deadness in the church was rooted in a deadness within the Christian. Only the "power of the blood" could cleanse and renew the soul. The hymn that became synonymous with the revival

---

[10]Robins, "Tukutendereza," p. 140.
[11]Ibid.
[12]Ibid.
[13]Ibid., p. 145.
[14]Ibid., p. 146.
[15]Ibid., p. 147.

was "Tukutendereza Jesu" ("We Praise You Jesus") with its emphasis on the shed blood of Christ ("O, the cleansing blood has reached me"). The power of shed blood and sacrificial death deeply resonated with people whose own Bugandan religious traditions required the shedding of blood for ritual purity and whose own ancestors had died as martyrs for the Christian cause.

If the real problem lay within the human heart, then the way to church reform was the way of personal repentance and holiness. Joe Church wrote of a meeting held in Kenya in which he publicly revealed his struggle with sin. One of the many who responded to the message after the meeting explained his response by saying, "I have never before seen any white man admit that he had any sins!"[16] The theological basis for this revival practice of confession of sin through brokenness and walking in the light was an evangelical understanding of the cross of Christ and Keswick style holiness based on the cross.

Bishop Festo Kivengere, a revival leader in Kigezi in western Uganda, summarized the Balokole theology of the cross in 1974 at the Lausanne Conference. The condition of fallen humanity, he declared, was one of conflicting "pulls." The outward pull of things and broken relationships, the downward pull of violent appetites and passions, the upward pull of impossible ideals and the inward pull of emotions and ambitions. The cross, he argued, was where God entered into our struggle with all of these conflicting pulls and resolved these conflicts.

Quoting Galatians 4:4 Kivengere asserted that the cross resolves the upward pull of impossible ideals because it "ends our despair of ever reaching God through our futile man-made endeavors to goodness and providing the fresh and life-giving way to fellowship with God." It ends the downward pull because it goes to the "very roots of our depravity and helplessness." It ends the inward pull of self-centeredness by giving the person a "new and right center" and thereby "brings inner wholeness." The cross changes the outward pulls of things and broken

---

[16]J. E. Church, *Quest for the Highest* (Exeter, U.K.: Paternoster, 1981), p. 145.

relationships by removing the "conflicting elements" that stand between individuals and groups. Kivengere declared the theology of the cross to be "the hope for my beloved . . . Africa with all its conflicting problems."[17]

The work of the cross was more than forgiveness. The cross also provided the foundation for a holy life. Joe Church who was exposed to the Keswick message of complete surrender as a student at Cambridge believed that it was this model of holiness that produced the revival. "We never remember anyone coming to us . . . to hold meetings on revival or to preach to us about it. Revival is not a program but a way of life. A God-given hunger for more holiness and Christ-likeness has come upon us and what is known as revival followed."[18]

This emphasis on the cross and its power both to liberate the conscience and transform the life was the basis for "walking in the light" and its spiritual two-step of public confession and brokenness before God and others. The revivalists saw a threat to this simple message in the theological liberalism visible in missionary circles by the late 1920s. At a Balokole convention in 1941 a strongly worded resolution sought to protect the theological foundations of the revival. The revival movement must reject "modernism" because it "minimizes sin, and the substitutionary death of Christ on the cross, and mocks at the ideal of separation from the world to a holy and victorious life."[19]

WILLIAM NAGENDA AND THE MUKONO INCIDENT

Attending that 1941 conference was a former theological student, William Nagenda. He had just been expelled from the Bishop Tucker Theological College, the leading Anglican training school in Uganda. Many revivalists saw this crisis, known as the Mukono incident, as a

---

[17]Festo Kivengere, "The Cross and World Evangelization," in *Let the Earth Hear His Voice*, ed. J. D. Douglas (Minneapolis: Worldwide Publications, 1975).

[18]Church, *Quest for the Highest*, p. 126.

[19]Kevin Ward, "'Obedient Rebels'—the Relationship Between the Early 'Balokole' and the Church of Uganda: The Mukono Crisis of 1941," *Journal of Religion in Africa* 19, no. 3 (1989): 120.

confrontation between their new light paradigm of the cross and the anti-light paradigm of theological modernism.

William Nagenda was a son of a "prominent Ganda chief" and brother-in-law to Nsibambi. Trained at Makerere University, Nagenda had worked for the colonial administration. After his conversion through Nsibambi he left his job and looked for ways to be used to promote the new revival. After the sudden death of Kigozi in 1935, Nagenda, described by his contemporaries as "a brilliant and convincing preacher," filled the gap. His base of operations was the tea plantation of Leslie Lea Wilson, a revival supporter, who invited Nagenda to be a resident chaplain. From a base beyond the reach of church hierarchy, Nagenda intended to spread the message of revival throughout East Africa and beyond. But first Anglican ordination would be necessary to open doors through the region.

Nagenda decided to join the Bishop Tucker Memorial College in Mukono not only as a student but as an agent of renewal. He and his fellow Balokole initiated a 4:00 a.m. prayer meeting. They preached against sin and modernism at the college. The transfer of a prorevival English missionary from the college precipitated a confrontation between student revivalists and an antirevivalist administration. The warden, J. C. Jones has been described as a "liberal evangelical" with a "deep mistrust of the emotionalism of revival."[20]

Immediately after this transfer Jones ordered the prayer meetings and evangelistic preaching to cease. Nagenda and his supporters refused to recognize these restrictions and continued the revival practices. After a brief impasse, Jones dismissed twenty-six Balokole students from the college. One student burned his textbooks before his departure, explaining that they were "full of heresy."[21] Bishop Stuart called the expulsion "the greatest crisis in the history of the Uganda church."[22] Robins believes that this action "effectively terminated ef-

---

[20]Ibid., p. 202.
[21]Robins, "Tukutendereza," p. 154.
[22]Ibid., p. 155.

forts at the full incorporation of the Balokole within the church." Stuart feared that the revival contingent would split and form their own church. Back at his tea plantation base, Nagenda contemplated just such an action. Balokole supporters arrived at his home to pray and determine the next step. Would an *"Abalokole* church" be created? Bishop Stuart "publicly appealed for unity" but supported the anti-revival party with his actions.

Prorevival elements were strongly critical of the action by the Warden and the lack of action by the bishop. The bishop countered that the "rebels" received a fair treatment given their flaunting of the regulations. The debate moved, inevitably, from specific doctrinal or spiritual issues to the struggle over authority. The bishop passed a sweeping set of regulations intended to curb revival excesses. These included a ban of the revival practice of refusing baptismal candidates unwilling to publicly confess sin, favoring prorevival priests and deans when filling vacancies, and holding evangelistic meetings without Episcopal permission. Stuart barred Nagenda from preaching in any meeting or conference of the Church of Uganda.

The Balokole responded to Stuart by agreeing to stay in the church but only as a "witness against sin in the church." They rejected the totalitarianism of the new rules and the shabby treatment of the "rebels." They would send no more students to the theological college at Mukono. A memorandum was signed filled with criticisms of the church. Nagenda resolved to desist from preaching inside the church but traveled widely to speak at home meetings and outdoor conventions.[23]

The Synod of 1942 represented a hardening of position by the church. The bishop blamed much of the division on the Balokole while several antirevival church leaders agreed to banning all public meetings on church ground that were larger than twelve people. Communication between the rival factions broke down. Joe Church, a mediating force in many ways, lost his license to preach in late 1942. Growing opposi-

---

[23]Ibid., p. 157.

tion to the revival in Ankole and Bunyoro paralleled the increasing tensions in Buganda. Nagenda was targeted as a troublemaker whose meetings (in his own words) "brought 'wars' in their wake."[24]

The Balokole leadership opted for formal unity but spiritual separation. The revival leaders remained adamant that the Church of Uganda was in the wrong and needed to repent. Stuart insisted that the Balokole were disloyal. Revivalists countered that the church was unrepentant and dead. For the next twenty years, Nagenda and the Bugandan wing of the Balokole movement focused almost exclusively on evangelism and networking outside the Church of Uganda.

THE REAWAKENED

The Puritan impulse with the Bugandan phase of the revivalist created internal conflicts as well. The original Balokole movement was divided by the new politics and the new prosperity of the 1960s. In this context a new reaction against perceived laxity with the brethren produced the *okuzukuka* or reawakening movement. Leaders of the new movement became more puritanical and focused on the sinfulness of indebtedness, striking at the root of the new capitalism. "Characteristically," writes Robins, "the activities coming under attack were associated with a modern, essentially Western life-style, as this was understood in postwar Buganda."[25]

J. V. Taylor writes of the middle-class dynamics of evangelical revivalism in Uganda:

> The disconcerting fact is that Evangelical Christianity, with its Gospel of individual conversion, the good news of rescue and the power to be different, not only appeals to but also creates a bourgeoisie. The revival movement, for example, calls peasants and herdsman to rise above the muck, morally and spiritually. In a very short time they have inevitably risen above it socially. Money that was spent on drink or women or divination is put into the home. In a few years husband and wife are

---

[24]Ibid., p. 165.
[25]Ibid., p. 302.

justifiably proud of their house and garden, of their children, and of their reputation. Even the simple, older village women in the movement have a new outlook; in relationship to the peasant society. . . . A new class is being created, fashioned by the Gospel in alliance with modern enlightenment.[26]

This conflict over social and economic mobility reached a peak in 1971 when a complete break occurred. In 1970, six thousand Reawakened met in Kampala to show their strength. Nsibambi reacted angrily to the splinter group's treatment of Nagenda at one meeting. He was further enraged at their teaching that "brethren saved at university cannot be saved properly."[27] Nsibambi concluded that these extremists had fallen from grace and were to be rejected as part of the true Balokole. Similar conflicts in Kenya led to the marginalizing of the reawakening movement across East Africa.

KIGEZI AND CHURCH-BASED REVIVAL

The revival in Buganda was only one face of the East African revival. The movement in Kigezi, a Ugandan district close to the Rwanda border illustrates the movement's diverging paths in the years between 1935 and 1945. For many reasons the Kigezi wing of the revival was more successful in moving in and with the Anglican church at large and also more effective in engaging society. Dreams and visions seemed to play a much larger role than in Buganda. "Visions, dreams, and extreme fear" soon spread in the area, giving rise to a condition of religiously inspired shaking or trembling known locally as *okukugusibwa*. Robins writes that "fear of damnation was a major element in the genesis of this condition."[28] By July 1936 Arthur Pitts-Pitts, archdeacon of the Rwanda Mission, reported "the spread of the revival on a very large scale in Kigezi and Rwanda." Importantly, it was traditional religion, rather than established Anglicanism, that was the major foil for the

---

[26]J. V. Taylor, *Growth of the Church in Buganda* (London: SCM, 1958), p. 257.
[27]Robins, "Tukutendereza," p. 372.
[28]Ibid., p. 233.

early revivalists in Kigezi. This would prove to be a major difference in shaping the two streams of revival.

What did the revival in Kigezi look like? Joe Church described one meeting he attended in 1939 in Ruzhumbura in northern Kigezi. Thousands were deeply moved, "prostrate, weeping and crying."[29] Many of those in attendance were from the ranks of the pagan Hima tribe. Joe Church described his counseling role after the preaching service: "We would divide up and ask all those who were weeping to stay behind, all those who weren't to go outside, and then we used to read texts about assurance. These people . . . often [had] a great fear of damnation."[30] The district commissioner commenting on the revival in the same region the previous year wrote that "the end of the world has been preached as a literal and terrifying phenomenon in the immediate future." Despite attempts to correct the eschatological hysteria, the "twice born are still pretty rabid."[31]

Unlike Buganda, the Kigezi revival became fully incorporated into the church. Robins writes that "the brethren came out of this [period] in Kigezi fully loyal to the Anglican church in the District, and to its servants, and prepared to cooperate with secular authority wherever its demands did not directly conflict with their religious obligations." Between 1940 and 1950 a full fusion between church and movement occurred that made it stand in sharp contrast to the Bugandan experience of revival. Leaders and clergy were actively integrated into the movement producing a "revivalist church." By 1946, in sharp contrast to Buganda "the primacy of the fellowship in the leadership of the church was almost complete and the legitimacy of the movement was unquestioned."[32]

How did the Kigezi revival impact society? Robins notes that missionaries tended to see the revival in "conversionist" terms but that lo-

---

[29]Ibid.
[30]Ibid.
[31]Ibid., p. 235.
[32]Ibid., p. 276.

cals saw it more as "ecstatic experiences and the redefinition of social reality." The new ethical code that arose from within the revival became "sources of conflict with the administration and with the unsaved of the surrounding communities." Some of the "secular" conflicts that the saved experienced were clashes with the colonial administration over night singing and the refusal to cultivate tobacco and refusal to pay money towards the new world war which had just broken out. There also were increased episodes of conflict between Roman Catholics and Protestants. Reports of persecution by Catholic chiefs were common. The revival brethren were against war in general and many refused military service. Socially, the traditional caste system in northern Kigezi clashed with revival egalitarianism. "From 1939 on," observes Robins, "Hima converts experienced radical changes in behavior and attitudes, penetrating most areas of their society." A social revolution was unfolding.

The same economic and political developments that divided the revival in Buganda characterized Kigezi in the 1950s and 1960s. In contrast to the Buganda revival, the 1960s saw a "second revival" which restored core values without factionalism. "The brethren have emerged from this period strongly committed to a complex of religious values which are identified with an essentially 'progressive economic and social ethic, and the movement has come to play a central role in the life of the district.'"[33] The year 1971 also saw a new time of repentance from factionalism and tribalism that stood in contrast to the permanent rupture of the brethren in Buganda. The Kigezi leadership flatly rejected the teaching of *okuzukuka* in 1966 and avoided the kind of confrontation and split that affected Kampala. It is significant that the most effective pan-African Christian leader of the revival after the Amin years was the bishop of Kigezi, Festo Kivengere (1919-1988).

Kivengere was a teacher in Kigezi on his way home drunk from a party when he was confronted by a "saved" friend. Her simple testi-

---

[33]Ibid.

mony led to repentance and new faith. In 1946 he went to Dodoma, Tanzania as a missionary educator. He returned to Kigezi four years later. After completing studies at London University and Pittsburgh theological seminary he returned to Kigezi and was ordained a priest and eventually a bishop. Kivengere continued his work as an evangelist, forming the African Evangelistic Enterprise (a branch of African Enterprise led by South African evangelical Michael Cassidy) which worked for both racial reconciliation and reconciliation with God through Christ. Whereas most of the revival leaders in Buganda were outside the established church, the situation in western Uganda as typified by Kivengere, was different. The revival became part and parcel of church life and restored a missional vision to Anglicanism in Uganda and beyond.

The revival entered Ugandan Independence united in its core paradigm of walking in the light but deeply divided about how that paradigm applied to the Church of Uganda. Reawakened zealots were critical of other Balokole who did not separate sufficiently from church and world. Bugandan revivalists of the Nsibambi and Nagenda variety focused on staying within the church as a critical presence and accusing conscience. The Kigezi brethren mainstreamed the revival into existing church structures and avoided the church-revival cleavage that characterized the other groups. Because global revivals need effective organizations in order to flourish, we need to turn our attention to the question of which of the various approaches was most effective in producing the new wineskins for the new wine of radical holiness.

RATIONAL CHOICE THEORY AND HIGH-TENSION CHURCHES

The East Africa revival had little direct impact on the social and political questions of both pre- and post-independence Uganda and East Africa. There was no discernible program of social or political engagement. It is true the revival leaders like Anglican Archbishop Janani Luwum were martyred by Amin in the 1970s and that many revivalists lost their lives in the highlands of Kenya when they resisted the Mau

Mau movement in the 1950s. Yet this fact about the revival seems to contradict our working definition of revival from chapter one that revivals are *charismatic people movements that seek to change their world by the translation of Christian truth and the transfer of power.* How did East African revivalists seek to change their world?

In later chapters we will note that "real world change" can involve a change in *status* (a people gains a new empowering identity), *structures* (new ways to be the church) and *systems* (social, economic, political change). Seen from this perspective the East Africa revival changed the colonial world situation of Uganda and surrounding countries for tens of thousands by changing their status and offering new structures that reinforced their new identity. People were no longer simply the colonized. They were the "Awakened Ones" or "Those on Fire." They were the "saved."

From that new status came a change in structures. The greatest legacy of the revival was the creation of radical community within and around the Church of Uganda and similar mission churches in the region. Writes Kevin Ward, a leading historian of Ugandan Christianity and the Balokole movement: "The *Balokole* Revival has had a deep impact on many of the Protestant churches of Eastern Africa, invigorating and renewing their life and offering to individuals the challenge of a deeper experience of salvation in Christ and a more radical commitment to Christian discipleship."[34]

This contribution is not a small one. In one sense we could say that the revival helped to decolonize the historic churches during these crucial decades, enabling them to stand on their own apart from state control, support or opposition. How this happened illustrates the producing of radical community as part of the life cycle of a global revival. To show what this radical community looks like we need to take a detour into religious sociology.

Ernst Troeltsch famously divided churches into two types based on

---

[34]Ward, "Obedient Rebels," p. 113.

their view of society.[35] The "church" type was a church that was part and parcel of the society, committed to providing spiritual support for the state and society. Membership into a "church-type" church was usually infant baptism which allowed such churches to grow by natural birth. The second type was very different. "Sect-type" churches were more demanding. They usually expected members to join after a conversion experience. They demanded a level of volunteerism and discipleship not required in the church-type fellowships. Over time, said Troeltsch, due to the passing of the founding generation, most sect-type churches will turn into church-type churches. They will modify their particular mission and embrace the wider mission of the society and state. They turn from being critics of the status quo into stakeholders in the status quo.

Other sociologists prefer to speak of "churches of choice" versus "churches of place." Secularization will often turn a church of choice into a church of place as it adjusts itself to the expectations and agenda of the general culture. Troeltsch assumed that secularization was inevitable and unstoppable. Sect-type churches in his schema were doomed to marginality in a world in which the only way a church could survive without losing their minds or their members was by serving the social agenda of the society.

But what if secularization is not inevitable? What if it is merely an exception rather than a norm? What happens to the church when a society undergoes desecularization? What happens in a society in which no one church has a religious monopoly? Can churches of place turn into churches of choice demanding new forms of mission, discipleship and morality not traditionally demanded? Troeltsch doubted very much if that could happen. For many sociologists like Troeltsch the movement from church to sect would be irrational, since it would mean rejecting the dominate worldview and value system of the society and living in "cognitive dissonance" that could not be sustained for long

---

[35]Ernst Troeltsch, *The Social Teachings of the Christian Church*, 2 vols. (New York: Harper & Row, 1960).

against dominant views. Cognitive dissonance is a polite way to call someone crazy. But Troeltsch and his followers knew little about global revivals.

Rodney Stark, a sociologist of religion, argues that Troeltsch was wrong. People join sect-type movements or seek to turn their church into more of a sect-type fellowship not because they are crazy but rather because they are rational. Stark suggests that human beings approach religion much as they approach other aspects of life—as rational people seeking the best value possible in all areas of life. Since Christian revitalization movements are religious in nature, the definition of religion matters. But what is religion? For Stark and Finke, "religion consists of very general explanations of existence, including the terms of exchange with a god or gods."[36] People tend to act in ways that maximize benefits to themselves and their families. When it comes to religion, people do the same. They look for the best value. Rather than seeing religion as the sum of all things irrational, such as "an illusion" (Freud), "a projection of nature" (Feuerbach) or an "opiate" that paralyzes people in inaction (Marx), the religious behavior of most people over most of history has been rationally pragmatic. People seek rewards that only the gods are perceived to offer and consequently seek to get these rewards at the best price. Once a religion's general explanation of existence is accepted as valid, this explanation becomes the rational framework within which the exchange takes place. People are willing to "pay" more (radical commitment, voluntary service, martyrdom) if they can get more (salvation, eternal life, union with God, victory over evil, sin and the grave, etc.). This is why liberal churches which tend to demand less of participants will lose members over time. They do not offer enough in terms of assurance of salvation, of life after death, of union with God, of ultimate meaning and purpose. Conservative churches tend to grow over time because they offer more and can therefore demand more of their members. For rational

---

[36]Rodney Stark and Roger Finke, *Acts of Faith: Explaining the Human Side of Religion* (Berkeley: University of California Press, 2000), p. 91.

people, evangelical churches are a better deal than liberal churches because they offer a greater value for investment.

In light of rational choice theory, Kigezi produced the most radical community in revival terms. While leaders like Bishop Kivengere produced new mission agencies like African Evangelistic Enterprise they did so from a strong foundation in a revitalized church. Kigezi revivalists moved the Church of Uganda away from a church-type organization that existed to bless the standing order and more towards a sect-type church that raised the costs of being an Anglican Christian (conversion, activism, repentance) by increasing the rewards offered (assurance of salvation, personal liberation, revitalized faith, new mission and purpose, etc.). The other streams of the revival made these kind of demands on their revival fellowships but remained either so marginal or so divided from Anglican leadership that they did not enjoy the kind of structural renewal that was seen in Kigezi. Kigezi used the revival to turn the church into a missional structure. The other branches used the revival to provide an alternative missional structure to the church. Global revivals produce all of these variations but tend to have maximum impact when they help existing churches of place become revitalized churches of choice.

How did the three major streams of the movement (Kigezi, Buganda and the Reawakened) differ in their impact on church and culture? By including the revival leadership in the hierarchy of the church, Kigezi Protestantism became a dynamic and united movement that embraced social development. While the Bugandan stream of the revival and the Reawakened faction seemed to exhaust their energies protesting a colonial church, Kigezi embraced both social change and the Church of Uganda and revived them both.

What happens after revivals create radical communities? If a revival is more than local it may seek to link with other revived churches elsewhere. This networking that is such a large part of global revivalism brings us to our next case study, the postwar renewal of American evangelicalism and the construction of the global evangelical network.

6

BORN AGAIN

Billy Graham and the
Revival of American Evangelicalism

On a Memorial Day weekend in 1945 some seventy thousand Chicagoans gathered at the cavernous Soldier Field to commemorate Americans who had given their lives in the soon to be resolved world war. Patriotism, however, was not the only item on display. Just as significant for the capacity crowd crammed into Chicago's largest forum was the celebration of a new youth movement sweeping the country. Youth for Christ (YFC), marking its first birthday, was a national phenomenon, already holding large regular rallies in almost four hundred cities and towns across America with a combined attendance of almost half a million. On this Friday evening the enthusiastic crowd swooned to the music of the large orchestra, the five thousand member choir and the deep throated solos of George Beverly Shea.

The patriotic program featured war heroes, young cadets and patriotic nurses. It also included a missions program. Youth dressed in the costumes of the world reminded the Soldier Field crowd that beyond the war to save the world from fascism lay another mission for America—saving the world from sin. A young evangelist named Billy Graham called for a new revival to change America and the world. *Newsweek* magazine, the Chicago media and national newspapers covered the spectacle. William Randolph Hearst ordered his twenty-two newspapers to cover future Youth for Christ rallies. Within a few years YFC would boast a thousand Friday night rallies held around the country with a million young people in attendance. Evangelists for the youth organization were traveling around the world bringing the message of revitalized evangelicalism to some forty-six countries by 1950. For historian Joel Carpenter, "Youth for Christ was one of the most striking early signs of a rising new evangelical movement," a movement that "has remained a prominent factor in American life since then."[1]

During the war American evangelicalism took important steps out of their marginalized subculture towards the center. The National Association of Evangelicals (NAE) was formed in 1942. "New hope for a revival," writes Joel Carpenter, "was prominent in the message of the first conventions of the" NAE.[2] Harold Ockenga in his inaugural address as the first president of the NAE saw the war as a crossroads for the world. One path meant "a return to the dark ages" and the other "the rescue of western civilization by a . . . Revival of evangelical Christianity."[3] Many evangelical leaders across America echoed similar convictions. In southern twangs and broad Midwestern tones American religious leaders seemed to agree with Dostoyevsky that civilization had only two choices: God or nothingness.

Sixty years after the YFC rally in Chicago I attended an Urbana missions conference in St. Louis sponsored by InterVarsity Christian Fellowship. Over twenty thousand evangelicals, mostly university students, came from all over the world, eager to find their niche not in the mission of America but in the mission of God globally. We packed into the Edwards Jones Dome, home of the St. Louis Rams football team, and sat riveted to a satellite address by Bono of U2 live from a Dublin pub. He spoke with passion on the need to get involved with global

---

[1]Joel Carpenter, "Youth for Christ and the New Evangelicals," in *Reckoning with the Past: Historical Essays on American Evangelicalism from the Institute for the Study of American Evangelicals*, ed. D. G. Hart (Grand Rapids: Baker, 1995), pp. 354-56.
[2]Ibid., p. 360.
[3]Ibid.

debt relief, HIV-AIDs and world poverty, and we cheered as he spoke. Worship teams representing different parts of the world shared their music. Rev. Oscar Muriu of Nairobi Chapel gave a plenary address on how African Christians are reinventing global missions. Ajith Fernando of Sri Lanka was the featured Bible expositor. His well-crafted messages laid out in vivid color the missional implications of the book of Ephesians with its bold proclamation that God in Christ had broken through the cultural barriers dividing the world.

Between 1945 and 2006 something dramatic had happened to American evangelicalism. It had been transformed from an embattled American subculture to an international network that saw itself as just one part of God's global mission. How had this transformation happened?

For some observers the shift of evangelicalism from white reactionaries to a rainbow people of international vision and activism is puzzling news. Many are more attuned to the Americanization of global evangelicalism than to the globalization of American evangelicalism. A significant number of critics argue that the new world Christianity is little more than an American export, clones of a Christianity that has sold its soul to conservative politics, rapacious capitalism and unbridled consumerism.[4]

There is evidence to back this view. Some might even say the revival tradition itself is an American export rather than, as we are arguing in this study, a vast collection of indigenous movements that translates the gospel into its vernacular languages and local cultures. Who's right?

Like many American evangelicals of the Baby Boom, I grew up with Billy Graham, with "Just as I am" evangelistic campaigns, Bob Dylan's protest songs and cold war paranoia about godless communism. I did my high school and college during the turbulent sixties and saw evangelicalism stumble as it tried to adjust to the cultural revolution that gave America, according to journalist Tom Wolfe, its fifth freedom:

---

[4]Cf. Adrian Hastings, "Clash of Nationalism and Universalism," in *Missions, Nationalism and End of Empire,* ed. Brian Stanley and Alaine Low (Grand Rapids: Eerdmans, 2003).

not freedom of religion but freedom from religion.[5] I saw the rise of reactionary fundamentalism in the eighties and the seduction of evangelicalism by the Republican revolution. American evangelicalism became obsessed with America, obsessed with saving it from this fifth freedom and the liberals and secularists who were perceived to be pushing it from Washington, Hollywood and New York.

Much attention has been paid to evangelical political influence in America. In light of the new world Christianity, however, I believe the bigger story lies elsewhere. The story I want to tell in this chapter is about a postwar American evangelical revival that not only created a new international network linking emerging centers of global evangelicalism but was also transformed in the process. I wish to argue that the key to understanding North Atlantic evangelicalism in America is not Washington but Lausanne, Switzerland, and the network that began there.

Stated more bluntly: the real significance of the postwar revival of American evangelicals lies less in its attempt to grab power in the West and more in its transfer of power to the evangelical movements of the non-West. If this sounds counterintuitive to the reader, then you are in good company. Researcher Jon Stone has documented the identity crisis of American evangelicalism. Over the decades it has lost almost all of its boundary markers, defining commitments that separate it from fundamentalism on the one hand and liberalism on the other.

What Stone missed in his boundary analysis was one of the most significant markers of evangelical religion: its sense of mission to the world. This is perhaps the one defining feature that has been strengthened, rather than weakened, by its contact with modernity. American evangelicals, like their Korean counterparts in the revival of 1907, underwent an unsettling globalization that produced a powerful glocalization. As it moved around the world, the North American revival actually gave away more power than it garnered and created an interna-

---

[5]Mike Burns, "Morality the Focus for Wolfe," *Ethics Classroom*, April 6, 2005 <www .ethicsclassroom.info/Archive.aspx?ADID=121>.

tional network that linked together a world full of local revivals to create a great and global awakening.

THE DRAMA OF AMERICAN EVANGELICALISM

The story of evangelicalism and revivalism in America hardly begins on that Memorial Day in 1945 when Billy Graham addressed the crowds in Chicago. Before there was an American nation there was an American evangelicalism.

Historian Timothy Smith called modern evangelicalism a kaleidoscope because of its penchant for change and renewal. "In virtually every successive decade since the year 1700," writes Smith, "the emergence of new spiritual movements, the regrouping of old alliances, and the effort to respond biblically to current moral and political challenges have produced significant changes in the pattern of North American Protestantism."[6] Rooted in the Protestant Reformation, American evangelicalism came to birth in the 1740s in the Great Awakening, a coalition of local revival movements in North America, Europe and Great Britain that laid new stress on the necessity of the new birth, the authority of the Bible, the centrality of the cross and the necessity of evangelism and social action.[7] Associated with names like Jonathan Edwards, George Whitefield and John Wesley, evangelicalism became a powerful transatlantic revival challenging enlightenment religion in the age of reason.

Soon after they burst upon the scene, evangelicals in America were quickly beset by revolutions at home and in France, hostile ideologies like deism and rationalism, and a host of complex social issues such as

---

[6]Timothy Smith, quoted in Jon R. Stone, *On the Boundaries of American Evangelicalism: The Postwar Evangelical Coalition* (New York: St. Martin's Press, 1999), p. 5.
[7]Cf. the discussion of this definition of evangelicalism in David. W. Bebbington, *The Dominance of Evangelicalism: The Age of Spurgeon and Moody*, A History of Evangelicalism (Downers Grove, Ill.: InterVarsity Press, 2005). For an authoritative and readable account of the origins of American evangelicalism see Mark Noll, *The Rise of Evangelicalism: The Age of Edwards, Whitefield and the Wesleys*, A History of Evangelicalism (Downers Grove, Ill. InterVarsity Press, 2004).

slavery, industrialization and poverty. The new movement regrouped in the early nineteenth century during the Second Great Awakening which witnessed evangelicalism's expansion across the new nation and the world, even as it plunged deeply into the greatest social crisis of the day, African enslavement.[8]

Surviving the American Civil War, evangelicals entered the "gilded age" stronger than ever, producing what Martin Marty has called the "Righteous Empire."[9] Spurgeon in England and Moody in America were just a few of the public faces of evangelicalism, but its popularity expanded in the last half of the nineteenth century despite the rise of atheism, evolution, Marxism, Freudianism and nihilism, views which challenged the very foundations of the faith.

Hidden beneath the public victories were private defeats, however, as Moody-style evangelicalism retreated from intellectual life, social engagement and holistic mission.[10]

Only in the twentieth century did these private defeats become public. Evangelicals in both America and Britain were in serious retreat. Secularists spoke of the inevitable decline of religion and a new enlightenment in which science would become the new orthodoxy. Liberal Christianity stepped in just as evangelicalism receded. Its main appeal was its attempt to move beyond a discredited evangelicalism and adapt the faith to modernity. Liberal Christianity defined itself in opposition to fundamentalism, the reactionary movement of disenfranchised evangelicals recoiling from their loss of power in church, state, academy and society. The Scopes trial of 1925, broadcast nationally on the radio, brought public humiliation to the fundamentalists who were forced out of the mainstream of American culture only to go underground, kept alive by their subculture of Bible

---

[8]John Wolffe, *The Expansion of Evangelicalism: The Age of Wilberforce, More, Chalmers and Finney*, A History of Evangelicalism (Downers Grove, Ill.: InterVarsity Press, 2006).

[9]Martin Marty, *Righteous Empire: The Protestant Experience in America* (New York: Dial, 1970).

[10]For the important story of evangelical transformation, see Bebbington, *Dominance of Evangelicalism.*

schools, churches and mission agencies.[11]

The evangelical revival after the war is all the more remarkable given this history of past glory and modern humiliation. The story after 1945 moves from an early stage of nationalism (tied to the recent past of God and country) through the secularist challenge of the 1960s (freedom from religion) to the resurgent 1970s in which an international evangelicalism is born and world Christianity becomes a visible movement.

OF GOD AND COUNTRY

Is postwar evangelicalism an expression of America's civil religion, a religious ideology justifying the moderate fascism trumpeted in William Randolph Hearst's newspaper empire and embodied in such cultural icons as Charles Lindbergh? Segments of the media in the 1940s raised this question and grilled YFC leaders for answers. Torrey Johnson's response was representative. Rejecting any political agenda, Johnson claimed that evangelicals had two goals only: "the spiritual revitalization of America" and "the complete evangelization of the world in our generation."[12] These were the twin goals, in various forms, that had characterized evangelicalism dating back to the Great Awakening. Grant Wacker calls these goals "the custodial ideal" and "the plural ideal." The former (America's spiritual revitalization) and the latter (world evangelization) had been knocked out of balance, argues Wacker, by the aggressive secularization of the 1920s. Johnson's claim rings true. Evangelicals were not joining any particular political party. They were simply finding new ways of being themselves.[13]

First came the mission to America. How could a movement so com-

---

[11]Two excellent studies of this period of evangelicalism that complement each other are George Marsden, *Fundamentalism and American Culture*, new ed. (New York: Oxford University Press, 2006), and Joel Carpenter, *Revive Us Again: The Reawakening of American Fundamentalism* (New York: Oxford University Press, 1999).

[12]Carpenter, "Youth for Christ and the New Evangelicals," p. 367.

[13]Grant Wacker, "Uneasy in Zion: Evangelicals in Postmodern Society," in *Reckoning with the Past: Historical Essays on American Evangelicalism from the Institute for the Study of American Evangelicals* (Grand Rapids: Baker, 1995).

pletely humiliated in the 1920s with the fiasco of the Scope's trial and the torrent of negative media coverage that came in its wake be given yet another chance to replenish American civil religion in the years after the war? The national mood was changing in the 1940s. The secular confidence of the 1920s had been shattered by the Great Depression of the 1930s when the validity of American democratic institutions was called into question. The recovery of industry and employment during the war years promised to restore the luster and credibility of the American Dream. With a great war to fight Americans from all ranks seemed eager to use the resources of religion to help win the war.[14]

Fundamentalists were not at all sure, however, that they wanted to return to the American mainstream on secular terms. One fundamentalist complained that while American God and country types were chanting about "praising the Lord and passing the ammunition," the truth was more like "passing the Lord and praising the ammunition." Yet these old light fundamentalists no longer spoke for the young evangelicals who had grown up during the war and who found their voice at the rallies sponsored YFC. The young leaders of YFC gloried in the new youth culture and its cult of celebrity. When YFC leader Torrey Johnson was called by *Newsweek*, "The religious counterpart to Frank Sinatra," there were no protests from his side. Billy Graham was billed, somewhat less glamorously, as the spiritual equivalent of newsman Walter Winchell.[15]

Three important cultural trends that emerged during the war were "a rising concern about youth and public morality, an increase of popular religiosity, and the renewal of American civic faith."[16] YFC in particular and the larger evangelical revival of which it was an important part responded to those trends positively, seeing a new opportunity for evangelical resurgence in the changed mood of the nation. YFC was

---

[14]Carpenter, "Youth for Christ and the New Evangelicals," p. 362.
[15]Ibid., pp. 362-63.
[16]Ibid., p. 364.

but the most youthful face of the new evangelical coalition. Billy Graham quickly emerged as the public face of this broader coalition, presiding over prayer breakfasts in the nation's capital and advising presidents in the White House. By 1956 they had a new voice, *Christianity Today,* which within a few decades would become one of the most successful religious periodicals in American history. Young evangelical scholars were graduating with Ph.D.s from the nation's leading universities. The long shadow of fundamentalism was receding and an evangelical renaissance seemed about to begin.

Leading this renaissance was the tall, willowy figure of Billy Graham. "As Graham went, so went the movement," observed Carpenter with little exaggeration.[17] Born in 1918 on a farm just outside Charlotte, North Carolina, Graham grew up in a strict Presbyterian home. He experienced an evangelical conversion as a teenager in 1934 at a "revival" meeting led by Mordecai Ham. Graham attended Bob Jones University but found it too legalistic and eventually graduated from Wheaton College in Wheaton, Illinois. During his Wheaton years he resolved his doubts about biblical authority under the influence of Henrietta Mears.

In quick succession Graham became a pastor, radio speaker, youth evangelist and college president by thirty years of age. He was best known to the postwar generation as the cofounder of Youth for Christ and then in 1950 as founder of the Billy Graham Evangelistic Association (BGEA). In the so-called Modesto Manifesto Graham and his team of evangelists pledged to avoid the scandals that had so tarnished other evangelists. Evangelistic work in Los Angeles (which attracted the attention of Hearst newspapers and *Time* magazine) won him national fame. Beginning with a controversial visit to President Truman (the press plastered Graham's picture kneeling in prayer on the White House lawn, much to the outrage of Truman), Graham would be the spiritual counselor of presidents and leaders around the world. His

---

[17]Ibid., p. 371.

marriage to Ruth Bell, daughter of missionaries to China, completed his early credentials as an evangelical leader.[18]

Graham in the 1950s represented the "niceness" of postwar evangelicalism. Rejecting the angry reactionary grump that was fundamentalism, the new evangelicalism sought to find a niche in the public arena without creating too much offense. If America was against communism, then so were the evangelicals. The young revivalists were negotiating their place at the national table and were not driving a particularly hard bargain. Just when they thought they had their deal, the sixties came and hit America and the new movement like a Normandy invasion.

"American public life encourages a facile tolerance," observed Joel Carpenter, "but tends to absorb, approve, and domesticate traditions and movements on previously established, safe cultural terms."[19] Like other global revivals we have studied, Billy Graham and the new evangelical revival of the 1950s moved quickly through the stages of leadership transfer and truth translation to the transformation of the world. By the late 1950s they were moving into the power stage, ready to make an impact in an America terrified by the cold war and communism. What happened next caught Graham and his movement off guard. Just as they found in anticommunism a gateway back into the cultural mainstream, the culture shifted. They tentatively moved into the 1960s completely unprepared for the new challenges that would rock them and most of America.

THE WATERSHED OF THE 1960S

A combination of forces unleashed in the 1960s conspired to erode enthusiasm for evangelism and mission. Liberal theology rejected the historical claims of Christianity. American social issues like civil rights, Vietnam and poverty raised the question of evangelism's relevance. An-

---

[18]William Martin, *A Prophet with Honor: The Billy Graham Story* (New York: Harper, 1991) remains one of the best biographies of Graham to date.

[19]Carpenter, "Youth for Christ and the New Evangelicals," p. 375.

ticolonial backlash in the Third World repudiated the missionary enterprise as the religious face of colonialism. Many mainline denominations called for a "moratorium on missions." Graham came under new attack not just from his fundamentalist critics but from the cultural elite. Winning people to Christ through personal evangelism seemed in bad taste.[20] With the strange new world of sexual freedom, civil rights and radical politics sweeping youth culture in the sixties, Graham struggled to remain relevant. In a way that had not been true before, he took up Torrey Johnson's second goal: The evangelization of the world. In that new pursuit he found a new ally.

Pentecostalism embraced Graham and the new evangelicalism emerging after World War II largely due to the latter's break with fundamentalism. Fundamentalism and dispensationalist views were hostile to charismatic insistence on signs and wonders, and argued that miracles had ceased during the time of the apostles. "In 1928 the WCFA [World Christian Fundamentals Association] rejected the Pentecostals as 'fanatical' and 'unscriptural,'"[21] In contrast the National Association of Evangelicals (1942) accepted Pentecostals and rejected the cessationism and separatism of the fundamentalists. The rise of the charismatic movement within existing denominations in the 1960s further enlarged the evangelical umbrella.

Another reality was operative in the late 1960s and early 1970s. Third World churches were growing and "were coming to see themselves not only as receivers but as senders of missionaries."[22] Despite the numerical resurgence of evangelical Christianity, what was missing "was a firm sense among Evangelicals that they were part of a coherent worldwide movement."[23]

In 1966 Billy Graham sponsored a conference in Berlin to plot new strategies of evangelism in the strange new world of postmodernity.

---

[20]Martin, *Prophet with Honor*, p. 440.
[21]Stanley M. Burgess and Eduard M. Van Der Maas, *The New International Dictionary of Pentecostal and Charismatic Movements* (Grand Rapids: Zondervan, 2002), p. 615.
[22]Martin, *Prophet with Honor*, p. 440.
[23]Ibid., p. 441.

Few if any non-Westerners were invited. The meetings were nonetheless deemed a success. In the postconference evaluation, a number of key leaders at Berlin encouraged Graham and his organization to consider an even larger and more representative "world congress."

By December 1971 Graham had put together the team that would lead the next conference. Leighton Ford was asked to chair the event. Donald Hoke, a missionary to Japan, was designated as the executive director with assistance from Stan Mooneyham, Jack Dain and Victor Nelson. The board of BGEA approved Graham's request to assume financial responsibility for the conference.[24] Despite the hostility of Western culture to evangelism in the sixties and seventies, pools of evangelical and charismatic renewal and revival were everywhere. What was needed was a network that connected the pools. Graham hoped that the next conference would do just that.

THE LAUSANNE BREAKTHROUGH

Time magazine in August 1974 wrote with some surprise that "millions of Christians . . . still believe that one of their foremost tasks is to preach the Gospel to the unbaptized."[25] As evidence, the article pointed to the extraordinary meetings held at a lake shore resort in Lausanne, Switzerland. Sponsored "largely through the efforts of the Rev. Billy Graham" the ten-day International Congress on World Evangelization with its twenty-four hundred evangelical leaders from one hundred fifty countries "served notice of the vigor of conservative, resolutely biblical, fervently mission-minded Christianity." *Time* was also quick to note that this "fervently mission-minded Christianity" stood in sharp contrast to the "prevailing philosophy in the World Council of Churches" with its offices a mere thirty miles away in Geneva. The magazine summarized the WCC's position on mission as the pursuit of "secular salvation, a human liberation in the political and social sense."[26]

---

[24]Ibid., p. 442.
[25]Quoted in ibid., p. 439.
[26]Ibid.

How representative would this new conference on evangelism be? Graham insisted on two issues. He would not make the Lausanne meetings an antiecumenical gathering. At the same time, Graham insisted that "every participant must be totally and thoroughly evangelical."[27] Executive director, Don Hoke, dreamed that Lausanne might be a twentieth-century Pentecost that would generate "a great spiritual fission whose chain reaction world wide will speed the completion of Christ's great commission in this century."[28]

Graham opened the conference with his keynote address. He noted the decline of evangelism in many of the historic churches citing the loss of confidence in the Bible, the preoccupation with social and political issues and the lack of strong theological commitment to evangelism. Graham hoped that the conference would reaffirm the authority of the Bible, redefine the relationship between evangelism and social action, and create a new kind of ecumenism, an evangelical one, characterized not by organization but by a common faith and a common mission. What about the American agenda and cold war politics, he asked? Graham sensed this question on the minds of the largely Third World audience in attendance. Repenting of his own practice in the 1940s and 1950s he declared that the gospel should not be tied to any political ideology. He promised that "when I go to preach the gospel, I go as an ambassador for the Kingdom of God—not America." The statement drew "warm applause."[29] The conferees sensed they were witnessing something historic, the creation of a worldwide evangelical movement. Bishop Festo Kivengere of Uganda and a leader of the East Africa revival, spoke for most when he observed that "you didn't have to say, 'They are one.' You saw it."[30]

A new concept was introduced at the conference, that of "unreached peoples." Championed by Ralph Winter and the Fuller School of World

---

[27]Billy Graham, quoted in Martin, *Prophet with Honor,* p. 442.
[28]Don Hoke, quoted in Martin, *Prophet with Honor,* p. 443.
[29]Martin, *Prophet with Honor,* p. 444.
[30]Ibid.

Mission, the concept of distinct sociological groups who are best reached by their own sons and daughters (designated E1 evangelism by Winter). In order to raise up E1 evangelists, E3 (radically different language and culture) must bridge the gap, create a beach head and then allow the dynamics of E1 to finish the task.[31]

But ripples of debate began to disturb the initial unity of the delegates. How can evangelicals around the world unite if the issue of social justice was not engaged? Two Latin American evangelicals, René Padilla and Samuel Escobar led the charge for a broader view of mission. Padilla was particularly critical of American evangelicalism's tendency "to identify Christianity with a politically and economically conservative middle-class American way of life."[32] Escobar added that American evangelicals tended to condemn "all the sins that well-behaved middle-class people condemn, but say nothing about exploitation, intrigue, and dirty political maneuvering done by great multinational corporations around the world."[33] In one of the most dramatic moments of the conference Escobar dared to contradict Graham. Graham had admitted his suspicion that concentration on social and political issues "would lead to the abandonment of the gospel."[34] Escobar's response was a defining moment: "I would like to affirm that I *do not believe in that statement.*" He went on to say that the decline of evangelism in the historic churches had less to do with social action than it did with bad theology. For Escobar authentic evangelism must not only declare that "the end is at hand" but must also engage in compassionate action "as evidence of our expectation of a new creation."[35]

Escobar served on the subcommittee, chaired by John Stott, which eventually drafted a fifteen paragraph "Lausanne Covenant." In one of its most critical statements it declared that "although reconciliation with man is not reconciliation with God, nor is social action evange-

---

[31]Ibid., p. 446.
[32]Ibid., p. 447.
[33]Ibid., p. 448.
[34]Ibid.
[35]Ibid.

lism, nor is political liberation salvation, nevertheless we affirm that evangelism and social action are both part of our Christian duty," adding that "faith without works is dead." Yet the drafting committee was divided over a phrase that made it into the final covenant. Comparing social action and evangelism, Stott inserted the phrase: "evangelism is primary." The Latino theologians demurred. The wording stood. Despite hedging on the part of the conservative elements on the committee the force of the covenant was dramatic. As William Martin observes: "The Lausanne covenant furnished Evangelical Christianity with a rationale for social action that it had lacked since the days of Charles Finney."[36]

The year after Lausanne Graham met in Mexico City to discuss the issue of some sort of ongoing organization. He was deeply touched by the Lausanne gathering and the voices of Third World evangelical leaders. He also confessed that the Lausanne covenant was the only "manifesto" that he had signed in all his years as an evangelist. At the same time he was against any kind of continuation committee that appeared to oppose the World Council of Churches. He also didn't want the movement becoming political. Meeting in January of 1975 at the Hotel Del Prado in Mexico City, Graham argued strongly that the newly formed Lausanne Continuation Committee "should stick with reconciliation with God" and not "get involved in all the things that God wants done in our generation."[37]

John Stott, an Anglican pastor, writer and evangelical statesman, whose role at Lausanne was second only to Graham's, disagreed with Billy. He insisted that the continuation committee should explore "the entire range of concerns" expressed in the Lausanne Covenant. Many of the gains of Lausanne seemed about to slip away. The debate was heated and the meeting ended late in the evening with sharp disagreement.

The next morning Graham met with Stott and the follow-up committee. To the amazement of all he had changed his position for the

[36]Ibid., p. 449.
[37]Ibid., p. 451.

sake of Christian unity. He agreed to a full commitment by Lausanne to a full-orbed mission. He further pledged to support the continuation committee financially through the BGEA. As one participant recalled: "I never witnessed a more magnanimous expression of tenderness and understanding. . . . What differences we had were largely resolved in an enveloping sense of trust and purpose."[38] The Lausanne Committee for World Evangelization (LCWE) was born. Ghanaian-born Gottfried Osei-Mensah became its first general secretary. A network was born and a torch was passed.

EMPOWERING THE GLOBAL SOUTH AND RENEWING THE GLOBAL NORTH

The importance of Lausanne for creating a global evangelical coalition was not always appreciated back home. Graham's own organization sometimes complained about the enormous cost of LCWE and its committee. The view from the Third World was more enthusiastic. Brazilian evangelical Nilson Fanini saw it as a "twentieth century Pentecost." Having traveled in over eighty countries after the conference, Fanini concluded that Lausanne revived "the spirit of evangelism and missions throughout the world."[39] They sensed history in the making. Without Lausanne the central role of international evangelicalism in the shaping of World Christianity would not be imaginable. Stott agreed. He noted with satisfaction later that the fires of Lausanne continued to burn as the century wore on. "What is exciting about Lausanne . . . is that its fire continues to spark off other fires."[40]

A GLOBAL AWAKENING

Postwar evangelicalism in America has redrawn the religious landscape of North America. Since 1960 the United Methodists have lost two million members, The Episcopal church, seven hundred thousand, and

---

[38]Ibid.
[39]Ibid., p. 455.
[40]Ibid.

the Presbyterian Church (U.S.A.) a half million. In contrast Protestant groups "all characterized by such labels as Bible-believing, born again, conservative, evangelical, fundamentalist, holiness, Pentecostal, or restorationist" have grown significantly. The best examples of this are the Southern Baptists. After a theological struggle in the 1970s and 1980s, conservatives gained control of the key leadership positions of America's largest Protestant denomination. With new theologically conservative leadership the denomination grew at a rapid rate "nearly 50% higher than the rate of national population growth."[41]

Despite its success, evangelicalism in the West continues to struggle with its sense of identity. Increasingly it looks globally for help in the midst of its identity crisis. International evangelicalism is even more complicated to define and yet in some ways its sense of common identity is stronger. Beginning in the 1970s at Lausanne and continuing up to the present with debates over gay ordination, American evangelicalism has relied more and more heavily on an international evangelicalism driven largely by voices of the global South to provide missional and moral boundaries that have renewed the movement's identity and forged a global coalition with renewed purpose centering on the revitalized vision of mission provided by Lausanne. Adrian Hasting, a persistent critic of American evangelicalism, was nonetheless impressed with the achievement of Lausanne. Crediting Stott's role at Lausanne, he wrote that "it was due to him that the Lausanne Covenant avoided a commitment to the verbal inspiration of Scripture [preferring the phrase "without error in all that it affirms"], made social action a partner of evangelism and stress . . . the collective responsibility of the visible church. None of this was very acceptable to main-line American Evangelicals."[42] By focusing on a mission core clearly defined in the Lausanne covenant, international evangelicalism found the elusive

---

[41]Mark Noll, *The Old Religion in a New World: The History of North American Christianity* (Grand Rapids: Eerdmans, 2002), p. 178.

[42]Timothy Dudley-Smith, *John Stott: A Global Ministry* (Leicester, U.K.: Inter-Varsity Press, 2001), p. 219.

boundary marker that had evaded American evangelicalism.

Under the banner of evangelical mission a big tent was created under which a host of local and global movements found sanctuary. In 1983, nearly ten years after Lausanne, Graham organized the International Conference for Itinerant Evangelists in Amsterdam. Pentecostals composed a significant percentage of the four thousand participants. In the year 2000 a second conference for evangelists drew more than ten thousand attendees. The Pentecostal and charismatic presence was even more prominent. The evangelical coalition globally as well as locally embraced Pentecostal and charismatic groups.[43]

What does the American evangelical awakening in the postwar era tell us about global revivals? Perhaps one of the most important lessons is how evangelical revivals tend to start with a parochial focus. They may display conservative tendencies that clash with forces calling for more radical change. Yet the powerful mission paradigm at the heart of Christian faith enables a maturing revival to move beyond the social and spiritual prescriptions of both old light and new light extremists. Grant Wacker rejects reductionist explanations of what he calls the "evangelical revival" in the postwar era. The problem with such explanations is that "they have assumed in short, that the revival has been an artifact, or epiphenomenon, of modern society, and that the fate of the former has been and will continue to be determined by the direction of the latter."[44] Wacker sees evangelicalism as a balancing act. On one hand they see part of their mission on earth as custodians of the moral and ethical fiber of the nation in which they find themselves. On the other hand they know they have been called to be a missionary people, calling no place home, but pilgrims carrying their founder's gospel into the crowded religious marketplaces of the world.

The decade of the 1960s knocked these two ideals out of balance. America was changing so rapidly that it destabilized evangelicalism's

---

[43]Burgess and Maas, *New International Dictionary of Pentecostal and Charismatic Movements*, p. 622.

[44]Wacker, "Uneasy in Zion," p. 380.

competing ideals: the custodial ideal of imposing a Judeo-Christian social agenda like ancient Israel and the plural ideal of embracing a theological diversity and multicultural mission like the book of Acts. In the period of destabilization a revitalized custodial ideal largely embodied in the American South went national and helped produce the new Christian right.

Wacker's approach is that American evangelicalism's relationship to modernity is difficult to label as either backward (historian William McGloughlin's view) or progressive (Martin Marty). For Wacker modern evangelicalism is best understood as a movement with both premodern roots and postmodern sensibilities. It carries within its collective soul the "custodial ideal" of the nation as a unity of religious values and public virtue. It is the ideal carried here by Puritans and maintained by revivals and Christian politicians: the conviction that public virtue is necessary for national life and that the church must hold the state responsible for its actions. The fifth freedom which calls for an abandonment of Christian morality and belief triggered an alarm that still reverberates through the movement.[45]

The American evangelical is haunted by a second ideal, however, which prevents her from simply focusing on moral rearmament. "Handcuffed to the custodial ideal," writes Wacker, is the "plural ideal." Simply put this ideal allows religious and cultural diversity in the public arena and anchors biblical faith in the private sphere of the individual and the voluntary society.[46] Just as the custodial ideal tempts the Christian to seize power, the plural ideal requires the sharing of power for the sake of mission and witness.

Wacker argues that the historic balance between these two ideals was upset by advanced modernization, a broad twister of cultural winds that meant that no one interpretation of public life, least of all a religious one, could exercise a monopoly in national life. In the 1920s the evangelical movement was dislodged from it privileged place in poli-

---

[45]Ibid., p. 384.
[46]Ibid., p. 385.

tics, society and the academy, and views more open to pluralism and diversity moved into the vacated spaces. Postwar evangelicalism, convinced that "American society cannot survive unbridled pluralism" fought back. The Christian right was born out of this rupture between the two ideals.[47]

I like Wacker's take on the uneasy soul of the evangelical in America. I have felt these same tensions in my own soul. In light of global revivals, I would add one additional footnote to Wacker's argument about the custodial and the plural ideals. The postwar revival was not only a destabilizing response to modernity but also a corrective response. In the 1970s, Billy Graham and his brand of evangelicals chose to move beyond the revitalized custodial ideal (read "saving my nation") into a revitalized plural ideal (read "blessing the nations") that helped forge a global network of international and culturally diverse evangelicals. As this network grew, global evangelicals, often products of local revivals, were granted an equal status in world mission and empowered to take an active role in a holistic mission to the ends of the earth. Ironically, the creation of this international evangelical network has helped give strength to the custodial ideal as American Christians struggle with the call for gay marriage and other social issues and have looked to Balokole African bishops for support.

Seen in this way the significance for world Christianity of the evangelical postwar revival has less to do with the rise of the religious right or the exporting of American religion than it does with the creation of an international evangelicalism, independent enough from its American component to be unique and yet connected enough to its common mission in the world to be a significant partner. Beginning with Lausanne and the unleashing of global voices, a Latin American evangelical social engagement, an East African revival piety of the cross, an Asian Christian quest for dialogue and witness in a religiously plural context, collided with American middle-class evangelicalism and al-

---

[47]Ibid., p. 387.

tered it forever. Though fundamentalists would grab the custodial ideal from the hands of Billy Graham and his new evangelicals, Lausanne ensured that the missionary and pluralist ideal of the book of Acts and the Great Commission of Christ was quickened. The two-way traffic on that broad and busy highway produced a great and global awakening that encouraged many new Jerusalems to become centers of holistic mission, even to the West.

The voices of Soldier Field on that windy Memorial Day in 1945 announced the twin goals of national renewal and world evangelism. Those voices, almost silenced by the sixties, almost drowned out by the angry shouts of the 1980s, have now become part of a global chorus reaffirming Torrey Johnson's twin goals on a global scale. Johnson simply had them in the wrong order.

7

SALT OF THE EARTH

Paulo Borges Jr. and Revival in Brazil

He was weaving in and out of traffic in the narrow streets. A cell phone in one hand and the steering wheel in the other, Paulo Borges Jr. carried on several conversations at once. We were on our way to Goiânia and to a reconciliation meeting with a Presbyterian church that had expelled Paulo Jr. twenty-five years before.

What had happened in the twenty-five intervening years since his expulsion? A revival happened. Paulo Jr. was swept up in a charismatic youth revival, part of a wave of revivals that moved through the entire continent in the 1970s. He quickly emerged as one of the young leaders of this revival in his city. The youth church that he and his rock band friends started included speaking in tongues and praying for miracles. Those were not something the reformed mother church was particularly approving of. When the dust settled in the late 1980s, Paulo Jr. was the head of a new movement in the city of Uberlandia, Brazil, a church movement known as *Sal de Terre* (SDT), Salt of the Earth, which numbered hundreds of churches in dozens of cities by the early 2000s.

I had traveled to Brazil to see the impact that SDT was having on issues like poverty, homelessness and youth crime in the city. I was looking specifically at the heart of global revivals—contextualization, a hunger in the heart of a revival to change their world in key ways. SDT was a microcosm of thousands of similar neo-Pentecostal churches that had been created by the third wave of renewal that swept over the Latin American continent in general and Brazil in particular in the 1970s. As I held on to the safety handle in Paulo Jr.'s weaving Range Rover, I recalled the story.

My trip to Latin America was a trip to a continent in religious ferment. Complicating the recent religious history of the continent is the influence of American political, economic and cultural forces for much of the twentieth century. As we heard in many of our previous chapters, the charge that Pentecostal movements are examples of "exporting the American gospel" of capitalism and conservative politics is a persistent one.[1] The fact that global evangelicalism and Pentecostalism seem to flourish under the very conditions of modernity and globalization that were supposed to spell Christianity's demise is seen as evidence of North American religious hegemony.

In this chapter I want to revisit my time with SDT and its founder Paulo Jr. and tell the story of Brazilian Pentecostalism. One of the things I want to look at is the authenticity question—are these movements Brazilian or foreign? Because of the very nature of revival movements as people movements that involve a transfer of power (the shift from foreign to local leaders) the charge that leaders like Paulo Jr. are simply expressions of the American religious right is unconvincing. The story of Brazilian Pentecostalism is the story not of an American export but a homegrown cluster of indigenous movements that translate Christian truth into Brazilian contexts in order to change their world.

These revival movements are producing churches that seek a political and economic third way that does not always fit neatly into the categories of either capitalism or socialism.[2] Like similar revivals in the

---

[1]Cf. Steve Brouwer, Paul Gifford and Susan D. Rose, *Exporing the American Gospel: Global Christian Fundamentalism* (New York: Routledge, 1996).
[2]For a discussion of democratic capitalism, cf. Michael Novak, *The Spirit of Democratic Capitalism,* rev. ed. (Boulder, Colo.: Madison Press, 2000).

West the social and political impact of Brazilian Pentecostalism is as unpredictable as it is varied.[3] Brazilian Pentecostalism is a story of revitalized indigenous Christians experiencing and expressing the kingdom of God in surprising and varied ways. The story unfolds in three waves. In each successive wave the three cultural dynamics of revival (the transfer of power to local leaders, the translation of truth into the worldview, and the transformation of the world through evangelical activism) will occur with increasing force and intensity.[4] I'll give special focus to wave three and how movements like Paulo Jr.'s SDT are changing both the religious and the cultural landscape.

WAVE ONE: 1910-1950s—BREAKTHROUGH AND BROAD APPEAL

The Brazilian Pentecostal story begins with a handful of adherents in 1910 but expands through the century to the point where Brazilian Protestants (*evangelicos* or *crentes*)[5] now compose an estimated 15 percent of the population (25 million) with about 70 percent being Pentecostals (17.5 million). This is by far the largest Protestant community in Latin America although growing movements exist in Guatemala, Chile, Nicaragua, Bolivia and El Salvador.[6]

Pentecostalism appeared in Latin America shortly after the famous Azusa Street revival of 1906. Freston notes that there were "Mexicans

[3]Cf. Laurence R. Iannaccone, "The Economics of American Fundamentalists," in *Fundamentalism and the State,* ed. Martin Marty and R. Scott Appleby, The Fundamentalism Project (Chicago: University of Chicago Press, 1993). Iannaccone explored the equation between North American conservative evangelical theology and conservative political and economic views. His research concluded that the equation is a myth.
[4]Key texts on the Brazilian Pentecostal and evangelical story include Paul Freston, "Contours of Latin American Protestantism," in *Christianity Reborn: The Global Expansion of Evangelicalism in the Twentieth Century,* ed. Donald M. Lewis (Grand Rapids: Eerdmans, 2004); R. Andrew Chesnut, *Born Again in Brazil: The Pentecostal Boom and the Pathogens of Poverty* (New Brunswick, N.J.: Rutgers University Press, 1997); David Martin, *Tongues of Fire: The Explosion of Protestantism in Latin America* (Oxford: Basil Blackwell, 1990); David Stoll, *Is Latin America Turning Protestant: The Politics of Evangelical Growth* (Berkeley: University of California Press, 1990).
[5]The Brazilian believers whom I interviewed all agreed that the term *crentes* when first used in the 1970s was a term of contempt. Over the last decades the term has gained new respect.
[6]Freston, "Contours of Latin American Protestantism," p. 228.

present at the famous meetings on Azusa Street." Within a few short years the revival spread to Chile, Mexico and Brazil.[7] Brazil seemed particularly receptive to the revival. Azusa Street was remarkable not only for the signs and wonders that occurred but also because racial divisions, at least for a while, were overcome under the influence of revival. This theme of racial acceptance and reconciliation has special meaning in Brazil, one of the world's most racially mixed societies. An estimated one-third of the population is so designated. Brazil imported over four million Africans during the centuries of the slave trade and their descendants have become a significant part of Brazilian life.[8]

In 1910 Pentecostal revival came to Belém, Brazil, in the persons of Gunnar Vingren and Daniel Berg, two Swedish Baptists from Chicago who were influenced indirectly by Azusa Street through the evangelist William Durham. Following a vision they came to Belém and formed a Pentecostal renewal group within the Baptist church. When one of the prayer group members, Celina Albuquerque, spoke in tongues and another member experienced faith healing, the small band was expelled

---

[7]Ibid., p. 224.

[8]E. A. Wilson, "Brazil," in *The International Dictionary of Pentecostal and Charismatic Movements,* ed. Stanley M. Burgess and Eduard M. Van Der Maas (Grand Rapids: Zondervan, 2002), p. 36. Three other features contributed to Brazilian preparation for Pentecostal renewal. One was the enlightenment impact. When Brazil became a republic in 1889 it was greatly influenced by progressive ideas emanating from Europe. One of those ideas was the dream of human utopia through progress and reason. This "quest for utopia" can be seen in the Brazilian flag. An abstract globe is emblazoned with the words "*Ordem e progresso*" (Order and Progress). A religion that was not only optimistic about the future but also taught the future was breaking into the present order was bound to attract the attention of masses of Brazilians. Yet another preparation came from poverty itself. Andrew Chesnut calls Brazil one of the "world leaders in socioeconomic inequity." Over 50 percent of all Brazilians are in severe poverty (a per capita income of half the minimum wage) and a quarter of the population lives in extreme poverty (one-fourth of minimum wage). Brazilian poverty extends to both urban and rural areas. One of the symptoms of poverty (the inability to meet basic human needs) in a society is the prevalence of illness (the misery that results from unmet needs). This illness is seen not only in poor health care but also in social terms (infidelity, spousal abuse, abandonment, alcohol and drug addiction). A final factor in the receptivity for the faith was Brazilian spirituality. Wilson describes the lush undergrowth of Brazilian spiritism expressed in Umbanda, Kardecism and indigenous spirituality as the "fertile soil" of Brazilian Pentecostalism. The fact that an estimated 85 percent of all Brazilian Protestants are Pentecostals is at least partly explained by this cultural soil.

from the mother church and formed the Apostolic Faith Mission. In 1918 the AFM affiliated with the Assemblies of God (*Assembléia de Deus,* AD) but in Sweden. In spite of persecution by both Protestants and the dominant Catholic Church, the new church attracted over a thousand adherents by 1930.[9]

Also in 1910, Luis Francescon, touched by the same Chicago renewal that had animated Berg and Vingren, founded the Christian Congregation (*Congregação Cristã,* CC). Originally attracting displaced Italians, the church eventually adopted Portuguese as its language of worship and broadened its membership.[10]

A third major church in Brazilian Pentecostalism was the Four Square Gospel Church (*Igreja do Evangelho Quadrangular,* IEQ). Founded in 1953 by missionaries from America as the National Evangelization Crusade, the IEQ was an urban phenomenon. Rapid industrialization in the nation in the 1940s and 1950s produced a mass exodus to the cities where slums swelled and unemployment skyrocketed. The IEQ held crusades in the slums of cities like Rio de Janeiro and São Paulo.[11]

This then was the first wave of Pentecostal renewal. Our model of a global revival stressed the importance of the message (the translation of Christian truth) in the early stages of a movement. What was the new light that Pentecostalism brought? Paul Freston sees Pentecostalism as essentially Protestant (for example, doctrinal, biblicist and evangelical). With David Martin he locates the movement within the older waves of Protestant dissent in the West (Calvinist, Methodist and Pentecostal) but notes that this third wave was more successful in penetrating the

---

[9]Chesnut, *Born Again in Brazil,* p. 26. Those who look for "the American Gospel" in Brazil sometimes overlook the fact that from early in the movement's history it has been Sweden and not the United States that has been the largest foreign influence. It should also be noted that Swedish Pentecostalism is much more socially and politically engaged than their North American cousins.

[10]Ibid., p. 30.

[11]Ibid., pp. 34-35. The new church grew initially but growth slowed as a new mood of nationalism demanded homegrown answers to economic, social and even spiritual problems. The emergence of populist nationalist leaders across the continent such as Vargas in Brazil, Cárdena in Mexico and Perón in Argentina turned their countries away from the global market and toward internal and regional economic solutions.

"Catholic societies of both Europe and Latin America." At the same time Freston argues that while it is essentially Protestant it is also "a distinct form of Protestantism" in which the experiences of spiritual rebirth and spirit baptism occupy a central place.[12] Freston again sees Pentecostalism as a collection of "conversionist sects" who seek to replace a "discharge of guilt and disease" with "a charge of power" leading to health and wholeness.[13]

The appeal of this new light, for researcher Andrew Chesnut, revolved around the treatment of illness. For many Brazilians, illness was physical, social, as well as supernatural. Conversion led the convert out of the world of sickness into a new world of healing. The stages of this journey were typically threefold. One moved from a sudden health crisis (on any of the three levels), through an encounter with God that resulted in faith healing to a final stage of "affiliation with the Pentecostal community." It would be a mistake to see healing only in physical or social terms. Supernatural healing was a critical third area of healing. Spiritual ecstasy through baptism in the Holy Spirit and the experience of charismatic powers enabled the believer to attack "the earthly vices that frequently culminate in illness."[14] This was the new light with which the revival began.

Despite resistance from the Roman Catholic Church in the 1940s who systematically persecuted these Protestant "sects," this gospel of healing and wholeness touched an immediate chord. Pentecostal numbers increased during these years of persecution. By 1949 both the AD and CC each had membership exceeding 100,000.[15]

WAVE TWO: 1950S-1970S—INDIGENIZATION, RESISTANCE AND GROWING IMPACT

During the Cold War that followed World War II, the United States

---

[12]Freston, "Contours of Latin American Protestantism," pp. 225-26.
[13]Ibid.
[14]Chesnut, *Born Again in Brazil*, pp. 23-24.
[15]Ibid., pp. 33.

moved aggressively to destabilize procommunist regimes in Latin America. One outcome of this was the rise of a number of military dictatorships (Chile, Brazil, Argentina). In 1964 Brazil suffered a military takeover. Both Pentecostals and Catholics, however, supported the removal of a moribund democracy. By 1968 the Catholics led by Dom Helder Camara and the National Council of Bishops reacted to their mounting membership losses by offering a "preferential option for the poor."[16] Pentecostalism continued to appeal to the masses even as it shifted to the right joining the Cold War opposition to communism.[17]

The time was ripe for the emergence of the first Pentecostal movement founded by a Brazilian. Manoel de Melo (d. 1970) had been a lay Pentecostal preacher before joining the National Evangelization Crusade. He soon became one of the most popular evangelists in Brazil. In 1955 he founded his own church, Brazil for Christ (*Brasil para Cristo*, BPC). Melo was one of the first Pentecostal preachers to make use of sports stadiums and radio.

Melo was also notable for his open endorsement of particular political candidates during the era of the populist-nationalists, backing such candidates as Ademar de Barros for president (unsuccessfully) and Levy Tavares for federal deputy in 1962 (successfully). When challenged about his involvement in politics Melo answered his critics using the rhetoric of spiritual warfare: "While we convert a million, the devil de-converts ten million through hunger, misery, militarism, dictatorship."[18]

---

[16]It would be a mistake to think that Roman Catholicism in Brazil has declined in the face of the evangelical revivals of the last century. Catholicism has experienced its own revival as Edward Cleary notes. Cleary credits Catholic resurgence not only to progressive bishops and the influx of Catholic missionaries throughout the continent but also to "numerous lay movements, including Catholic Action and the *Cursillos de Christiandad*" which "brought hundreds of thousands of lay persons into active roles within the church." The Latin Catholic Church which staggered into the twentieth century in decline had, over that turbulent century, "gained fundamental strength." The seminaries were full, indigenous clergy expanding, and a growing laity catechized and mobilized (Edward Cleary, "The Transformation of Latin American Christianity, c.1950-c.2000," in *Cambridge History of Christianity: World Christianities, c.1914-2000*, ed. Hugh McLeod [Cambridge: Cambridge University Press, 2006], p. 372).

[17]Ibid., pp. 40-41.

[18]Ibid., pp. 37-38.

Melo established himself as an outspoken opponent of entrenched Catholic power, communism, narrow religiosity and Protestant separatism. His embrace of an aggressive social program and entrance into the World Council of Churches set him apart from critics of both the right and the left. The denomination's fifteen-thousand seat flagship church in São Paulo is one of the largest church buildings in Brazil.[19]

In 1965 Melo participated in an ecumenical symposium in which a number of mainline church representatives met with fifty Brazilian Pentecostal leaders. The Brazilians were asked how their view of a "world full of supernatural and invisible powers" could provide material answers to the problems of poverty in Brazil. The Melo and Pentecostal pastors gave three responses.

First, they were the ones that "are in solidarity with the poor." Second, Pentecostal mission "does not confine itself to soul-saving." Third, they recognized the need for a wider "ecumenical context" to realize their full social impact. Melo was unabashed that Brazilian Pentecostalism was a restoration of the gospel unlike the compromised ideologies of the Western world. "Rome has brought to the world idolatry," Melo declared, "Russia the terrors of communism, the USA the demon of capitalism; we Brazilians, nation of the poor, shall bring to the world the gospel."[20] Although the AD remained the largest Pentecostal denomination in Brazil with its ten million members, Melo and his movement were in the top five with some five thousand congregations and one million members. Melo's revival gospel became more political and added insights from ecumenical perspectives.

Other second wave churches like God Is Love (*Igreja Pentecostal Deus é Amor*, DEA), founded in 1962 by Melo's brother-in-law David Miranda may be larger (three million members) but was less involved in

---

[19]Wilson, "Brazil," p. 40. After Melo's death in 1970 his son Paul became the head of the denomination and withdrew from the WCC. Cf. Alan Anderson, *Introduction to Pentecostalism* (Cambridge: Cambridge University Press, 2004), p. 73.

[20]Walter J. Hollenweger, *The Pentecostals* (London: SCM Press, 1972), p. 101.

social and political revitalization. Melo stands out as a symbol of Pentecostalism's search for a third way between the political left and right.[21] The Brazilian Pentecost was beginning to apply its vision of renewal more broadly.

WAVE THREE: 1970S TO THE PRESENT— NEO-PENTECOSTALISM AND ITS IMPACT

A new chapter in modern Brazilian history opened in 1978 with the return of limited democracy after nearly fifteen years of military rule. In indirect elections General João Baptista de Oliveira Figueiredo became president and declared his commitment to restore democracy to Brazil. Over the next decade democratic institutions returned but economic challenges remained including high unemployment and triple-digit inflation. The presidency of José Sarney in 1985 gave hope to millions, hopes that were quickly dashed as economic misery continued.

Andrew Chesnut calls the 1980s in Brazil the "lost decade." Domestic consumption declined by 25 percent and the number of Brazilians relegated to extreme poverty skyrocketed.[22] In many poor homes 20 to 40 percent of the family budget was spent on alcohol.[23] Chesnut attributed much of the domestic decline to the uncontrollable "rage of poverty." This rage was marked by a "profound sense of powerlessness, arising from the inability to properly shelter, feed, clothe, and educate themselves and their families." Additionally the male prestige complex

---

[21]Forsaking the "show business" style of Melo, Miranda avoided television but used radio to broadcast a stark message of personal holiness and unrelenting battle with the demonic through exorcism and deliverance ministries. While charismatic in character it is more conservative, even legalistic, in its teaching on personal morality and conduct. Spiritual warfare themes combine with strict dress codes to give this church its ethos. Miranda specialized in exorcizing by name the "gods" of Brazils most popular Afro-Brazilian religions of Candomblé and Umbanda. Chesnut claims he "raised syncretism to new heights." (Chesnut, *Born Again in Brazil*, p. 38.)

[22]Ibid., p. 56.

[23]Addiction to *aguardente* (fire water—the generic term for alcohol) means a "downward spiral of disease and poverty." This social disease is more common among men than women and is driven in part by what Chesnut calls the "male prestige complex" which includes work, soccer and sex (ibid., p. 57).

also "measures manliness partly in terms of sexual conquest." The infidelity spiral combined with shame over poverty led many men to abandon both their wives for younger women and their many dependents who amount to an unbearable economic drain.[24] It is against this backdrop of poverty and new disillusionment with the nation-state that the third wave of new religious movements in Brazil must be seen.

Many Brazilian poor tried other religions prior to becoming Pentecostals. There they experienced a feeling of "spiritual impotence." Pentecostalism alleviated this.[25] When Chesnut asked his sources to define Pentecostalism, they invariably said it meant "to be filled with the power of the Holy Spirit." Increasingly third wave Pentecostalism targeted the culture of the street with its evil spirits, drugs, unemployment, infidelity and violence and sought to transform the streets into sacred spaces. It attacked the root causes of "illness" and offered a comprehensive cure not dependent on the government. New converts entered a three-act drama of conversion (evil past, powerful encounter, entrance into new community) that transformed their lives.[26]

This promise of real change through Pentecostalism led to explosive church growth from 1970 to 1990. The new churches shaped by the conditions of the new poverty have been labeled neo-Pentecostal to distinguish them from the more classic Pentecostalism of waves one and two. The largest and most controversial of the neo-Pentecostal churches was the Universal Church of the Kingdom of God (*Igreja Universal do Reino de Deus*, IURD). Founded by Edir Macedo in 1977 the church grew rapidly in the economically turbulent 1980s. By the

---

[24]Ibid., p. 59.

[25]Ibid., p. 67. It is among the most impoverished citizens of Brazilian society that Pentecostalism has made the greatest inroads. Chesnut documents that Pentecostal churches flourish most in the poorest barrios (neighborhoods) based on data collected in both Belém and Rio de Janeiro. At the same time there is a notable economic lift for Pentecostal families after conversion. This is partly due to the elimination of expenditures on alcohol (ibid., p. 17).

[26]Chesnut elaborates this drama of conversion. Act one: "Without Jesus and the Holy Spirit, life before conversion was lived in the sinful world." In this period "disease, domestic strife and alcoholism" dominated family life. Act two means "the recovery of health" by accepting Jesus. Act three is "joining the church" which "means renouncing the world of disease and affliction for a life of spiritual and material well-being" (ibid., p. 51).

mid 1990s it had an estimated membership of between three to six million, had purchased a large television station, formed their own political party and bought a Rio de Janeiro football team. They expanded to forty countries. Yet for all of this expansion and investment, the majority of their funding came from the tithing of their own members.

While IURD leaders dressed and acted like secular celebrities, "They reject the key destructive indulgences—alcohol, tobacco, drugs, promiscuity—but retain much of the style."[27] Macedo preached an unabashed prosperity gospel and practiced mass exorcisms of Candomblé and Umbanda spirits during services. Boldly rejecting the legalism of classic Pentecostalism Macedo claimed that "we do not prohibit anything." Rather in his church "it is prohibited to prohibit." For example, "a man can have ten wives or a woman ten husbands." In contrast to older Pentecostal churches his followers are "free to drink, smoke, to do what they understand to be right."[28]

The Brazilian Christians I interviewed were all critical of the excesses of "Universal," as they refer to the IURD. Top among their criticisms were the highly controversial TV exorcisms, where IURD pastors would do live televised interviews with the "demon" possessing an individual. The ensuing exorcisms had all the signs of being stage managed. They also rejected the obsessive attention that televised "Universal" pastors gave to raising money. No large Brazilian neo-Pentecostal church pressed the prosperity gospel of health and wealth for those with enough faith as did the IURD.

At the same time the Brazilians I interviewed (representing three different churches) saw IURD as fulfilling a certain niche within Brazilian Pentecostalism. The church seems to be specifically targeted to those associated with Candomblé. In this African-based religion specific deities are worshiped, which are regarded as demons by most Pentecostals. Spirit possession and demonic oppression are widely reported by those associated with this Afro-Brazilian religion. The IURD takes

[27]David Martin, *Pentecostalism: The World Their Parish* (Oxford: Blackwell, 2002), p. 80.
[28]Chesnut, *Born Again in Brazil*, pp. 47-48.

careful aim at the widespread phenomena of possession by Candomblé spirits. Evangelists from IURD will even attend Candomblé meetings and challenge the "powers" that are said to possess the faithful.[29]

Yet these themes of exorcism, permissiveness and prosperity do not tell the whole story. Part of IURD's growing appeal was their multi-level attack on the causes of "illness," the evils of street culture. They emphasized deliverance ministries where strong prayer is offered to "destroy witchcraft, demon possession, bad luck, bad dreams, all spiritual problems," according to their website.[30] Most Brazilian poor believe in a supernatural cause of illness and poverty. Exorcism becomes a more relevant form of liberation theology for many because it moves beyond human causes of poverty (socioeconomic, political systems) and goes to the very heart of reality—the supernatural world and demonic attacks and offers relief on that level.

On another level the IURD gave their adherents a theology of hope that encouraged them to take risks and solve the problem of unemployment by becoming their own bosses. Though Freston notes that "Latin American Pentecostalism does not have a classic Protestant work ethic" he does believe that its spirituality of healing and hope encourages risk and entrepreneurship. He cites a typical IURD sermon: "It's no good just giving an offering. You must quit your job and open a business, even if it's only selling popcorn in the street. As an employee you will never get rich."[31] For impoverished and spirituality impotent Brazilians this message is a street-level liberation theology.[32]

---

[29]Interviews: Rilza Rodriguez/Montgomery, from Salvadore, Brazil, interviewed by author in Edinburgh, U.K., March 5, 2006; Emeric Vasvary, from Rio de Janeiro, Brazil, interviewed by author in Edinburgh, U.K., March 5, 2006; Marcy Vasvary, interviewed by author in Edinburgh, U.K., March 5, 2006. For a scholarly discussion of Candomblé cf. Mikelle Smith Omari, "Candomblé: A Socio-Political Examination of African Religion and Art in Brazil," in *Religion in Africa: Experience and Expression*, ed. Thomas D. Blakely, Walter E. A. van Beek and Dennis L. Thomson (London: James Currey, 1994).

[30]Philip Jenkins, *The Next Christendom: The Coming of Global Christianity* (New York: Oxford University Press, 2002), p. 65.

[31]Freston, "Contours of Latin American Protestantism," p. 266.

[32]One of the most questionable aspects of Chesnut's analysis of neo-Pentecostalism is his belief that millennial and eschatological thought plays almost no role. Chesnut reiterates at the end

While the large and controversial IURD grabbed the religious headlines smaller indigenous movements make up the greater part of third wave renewal. Many of these indigenous revival movements differ from the IURD theologically and socially. Yet the influence of Macedo's movement is undeniable. "Macedo helped to make Christianity Brazilian," observed one revival leader. "He broke the grip of European theology and dealt with Brazilian issues like witchcraft, spiritism and Catholicism" in a direct way that was not shaped by Western theology but still took the Bible seriously.[33] The IURD also showed other new movements how to "penetrate the city by invading secular space like using theatres as worship centers."[34]

Pastor Paulo Borges Jr. (b. 1957) and the *Igreja Christa Sal de Terre* (SDT) illustrate the diversity within contemporary neo-Pentecostalism. SDT also illustrates how the triple forces of theological inculturation, structural indigenization, and social and political contextualization play out in modern Brazilian revivalism. The SDT was born in the city of Uberlandia, a prosperous city of nearly six hundred thousand in the Brazilian state of Minas Gerais.

In 1971 Paulo Jr. experienced a dramatic evangelical conversion. As

---

of his study that millennialism had little or nothing to do with the rise of Pentecostalism as he had originally supposed. More surprisingly he discovered that poverty alone was not the driving force even in the face of the prosperity teaching. On the basis of his ethnographic research in Belém he claims that it is evil conceived as illness that is at the heart of the pentecostalization of Brazilian society. During its three stages of development, Pentecostalism became ever more adept at using media and other creative methods to deliver the fundament message and transforming vision of the movement: "Accept Jesus as your Lord and savior in our church, and you will be healed" (Chestnut, *Born Again in Brazil*, p. 168). Freston seems to question this. Durkheim's distinction between religion and magic is useful in studying Pentecostalism. Magic creates a clientele whereas religion creates a community. Chestnut's study, which concentrates so centrally on illness and healing as the key to understanding Brazilian Pentecostalism, might be cautioned about blurring this important distinction, although Freston does not mention this. Perhaps the distinction made in religious studies between religious phenomena as metaphor and metonym would help explain why Pentecostal power produces community rather than merely clients. When one sees healing as metonym, a part standing for a greater whole, the other realities of the gospel are affirmed and internalized (Freston, "Contours of Latin American Protestantism," p. 236).

[33]Paulo G. Borges Jr., interviewed by author in Goinia, Brazil, May 6, 2006.
[34]Ibid.

an adolescent he had been kicked out of several schools and was regarded as incorrigible by his frustrated parents. At a youth meeting Paulo Jr. felt his heart not so much strangely warmed as broken to pieces. Tears of repentance and a sense of forgiveness and cleansing flooded over him. Counseled by a seasoned Christian, Paulo Jr. recognized that he had experienced a "new birth." Out of this conversion experience Paulo Jr. sensed a call to ministry. During his university years, he and a group of friends including Cesar Peirera established a weekend ministry that they eventually incorporated as *Sal de Terre*.[35] Through the influence of an American missionary at a Christian camp, Paulo Jr. and his friends became charismatics.

In 1987, Paulo Jr. and his colleagues in the weekend ministry were given authority by the Uberlandia Presbyterian Church to plant a church in an undeveloped area of the city. This was one way to deal with the youth revival that was putting pressure on the mother church. By that time, Paulo Jr. had graduated from university with a degree in engineering and was working as an engineer in the city. His call to the ministry was strong, however. He and Cesar began the new church at Cesar's house. Paulo Jr. completed seminary training while working as an engineer. He eventually became ordained by the presbytery. The new house church grew rapidly and attracted many young people. A hall was rented to accommodate the growing congregation. In a just a few years it grew to five hundred with a school and an orphanage.

In 1989 tensions with the mother church reached a breaking point. The main area of contention concerned the neo-Pentecostal character of the new church. Paulo Jr. was called to a presbytery meeting and charged with teaching charismatic practices to his congregation. Saddened by this censure, Paulo Jr. resigned from the presbytery. He moved his young congregation to a new facility taking on the SDT name, already a legally registered entity. Soon the SDT expanded into three new congregations. New converts flocked to the new movement and it

---

[35]Alexandre Bastos, interviewed by author in Uberlandia, Brazil, May 2, 2006; Borges Jr.

expanded rapidly throughout the city of Uberlandia. The commitment to use only homegrown leaders, personally discipled by the founder or his close circle of colleagues illustrates the dynamic of indigeneity so characteristic of new religious movements.

The SDT also illustrate the dynamic of contextualization. Poverty, seen as both financial and spiritual, dominated the ministry agenda of SDT from its founding. Glocalization, the renewal and exporting of the local under pressure from social and cultural globalization,[36] is seen in SDT's commitment to reevangelize the United Kingdom. In the early 1990s SDT joined with a number of churches to found an inter-church missions fellowship called Go to the Nations. The original idea was to send Brazilian missionaries to the UK for training in English and local ministry and then partner with UK churches for further mission work in the Middle East and elsewhere. Paulo Jr. and most of the senior leadership of SDT spent 1994 and 1995 in Edinburgh and other parts of the UK establishing links and refining the vision. A British council was founded to work with the Brazilian council. A vision of reverse mission, the former mission field of Brazil focusing on the new mission field of a post-Christian Britain captured the SDT and plans went forward to establish permanent missionaries from Brazil in British churches in Scotland and England.

In 1996 Paulo Jr. was called back to Uberlandia by a crisis in the young movement. Several of the SDT pastors in the city, including one of the founders, resented the time and money being given to the UK mission effort and expressed their discontent. The Brazilian economy was experiencing runaway inflation in the mid 1990s. The government's inability to control the triple-digit inflation led to the introduction of a new currency in 1996. This move hurt millions who were unable to convert all of their old currency before the deadline. This national financial crisis affected the SDT movement in Uberlandia. Paulo Jr. was faced with the difficult decision of how to deal with dis-

---

[36]Cf. Roland Robertson, *Globalization: Social Theory and Global Culture*, Theory, Culture & Society (London: Sage, 1992).

sent and inner conflict. His solution was to offer the dissenting churches the option of financial independence for their congregation but the continuation of fraternal relations. Several of the dissenting congregations took this option and a split was averted.

Through the early years of the twenty-first century, the SDT remained a decentralized movement. It rejected a centralized, hierarchical structure in favor of a looser network characteristic of many neo-Pentecostal movements in Latin America. The bonds between churches are more organic than organizational as daughter churches link with a mother church while maintaining a much looser connection with the larger SDT movement. Such is the case with SDT's Centre West Church and its seventeen linked churches. This larger cluster of SDT congregations has made a major commitment to creative evangelism and mission. Between 2003 and 2006 fourteen new churches were planted.[37] This brought the total of SDT churches to forty-four by mid 2006. Yet the new coordinator of SDT and pastor of the important Centre West Church, Olgalvaro Bastos Jr., envisioned two hundred fifty new churches by 2015. Many of these churches will not be either among the traditional poor or middle class but among the new youth "tribes" of urban Brazil—punks, hip-hop and various forms of street culture. The vision is part of a Brazil-wide initiative called Tribal Generations and seeks to reach the segmented youth population of Uberlandia through rap, hip-hop, street dancing and a culturally relevant small group movement.[38]

Contextualization for the SDT has meant more than overseas mission and local church planting. The SDT has a strong commitment to the poor. I was able to see many of the programs SDT had instituted in Uberlandia to assist poor families and children. They run a clean and highly regarded orphanage, a home for young street girls, and several model day care centers. They run a program that builds houses for poor families, a dental clinic, an English language school, computer training

---

[37]Bastos.
[38]Olgalvaro Bastos Jr., interviewed by author in Uberlandia, Brazil, May 4, 2006.

program and a cultural arts center for teaching ballet, street dancing and other performing arts. All of these programs are aspects of SDT's vision to change the city using the resources of primal Christianity.[39]

The vision to alleviate poverty does not stop with housing and orphanages. In an interview with Pastor Marcos Rocha, a young protégé of Paulo Jr., I learned of SDT's larger political vision. SDT has actively campaigned for seats on the city council. One of the founding pastors of SDT, Cesar Periera, a university professor, became a member of the city government working to bring development to the impoverished neighborhoods of Uberlandia. They are committed to the election of evangelical Christian politicians on every level of government—city, state and federal. Rocha said SDT's vision is to see "godly politicians penetrating all levels of government over the next few decades," so that there will be a reduction in "the corruption that is hurting the country."[40]

While larger movements like the IURD show little interest in ecumenical ties with other churches, SDT is active in the cause of Christian unity. In 2004 Paulo Jr. handed over coordination of the SDT in Uberlandia to a capable younger associate, Olgavaro Bastos Jr. and moved to the city of Goiânia. This million plus metropolis, twice Uberlandia's size, has the distinction of being "the most Christian city in

---

[39]In an interview with pastor Marcos Rocha I learned more about the housing program. Rocha helped plant a church in a poor section of Uberlandia known simply as the Shopping Centre. Small groups were formed. As poor, unemployed families joined these groups they were adopted by the group. This involved a commitment to find school fees for the children and job training for the parents if they needed to find work. It also meant a commitment to help them build their own home. SDT would provide materials, money to purchase a lot and assistance in the building. Over thirty of these homes have been built through SDT in the city. The combination of evangelism, cell group solidarity and social development is an important part of the growth of the movement (Marcos Rocha, interviewed by author in Goiana, Brazil, May 7, 2006).

[40]Ibid. This is a sentiment I heard from the leaders of other neo-Pentecostal leaders as well new churches. Paulo Olvieiro Jr. , a former bank president and head of the *Igreja Christa da Familia* (founded in the 1980s and reorganized after a split in the mid-1990s) spoke of this vision for the transformation of Brazil from a country known for corruption and the gap between rich and poor. Like SDT they have a separate corporation to promote a host of social ministries *(Institutio Renovo)* but behind these ministries of mercy is a vision to reduce and reverse the corruption that is found on every level of Brazilian society.

Brazil."[41] Goiânia has been a center of neo-Pentecostal revivalism since the 1970s. New churches like the *Luz Para Povos* (Light of the people), *Videira* (Vineyard), *Communidade* (Community) and *Sara Nossa Terra* (Heal the Land), each numbering around ten thousand have a strong presence here as do older Pentecostal and evangelical churches from earlier periods of renewal. Disunity and rivalry is rife among these new groups and stories of personality clashes and wounded egos among the city's church leaders are common. Paulo Jr. moved to Goiânia to work from below to bring leaders together and forge new networks of *relationamento* (relationship). Several breakthroughs have been experienced. The Presbyterian churches of Goiânia have struggled to embrace many of the new movements including SDT which broke off from Presbyterianism. As unity is developed, SDT hopes to see the enormous human and material resources of the churches of Goiânia unleashed for development and justice.

Inculturation of theology is also a strong dynamic of the SDT. They would accept the mainstream theological tradition that is based in a literal and christological reading of the New Testament (primarily) as seen through the grid of the Protestant Reformation, evangelicalism and neo-Pentecostalism. Yet this evangelical tradition has been applied to the Brazilian world in which SDT lives and operates. The major social implication of this deeply internalized theological story is a powerful sense of inevitable progress and eventual success. If God is for us, who can be against us.[42]

Despite SDT's early success as a movement of revival, challenges remain. Like all revival movements, SDT faces, on the one hand, the challenge to avoid becoming a spiritual ghetto that is divorced from the real world. On the other hand they also face the danger of becoming a church so politicized that it is little more than an NGO concerned only with social aspects of the gospel. Like many of the churches of the third

---

[41]Duncan Wier, interviewed by author in Caldas Novas, Brazil, May 4, 2006.
[42]Luther Gerlach and Virginia Hine, "Five Factors Crucial to the Growth and Spread of a Modern Religious Movement," *Journal for the Scientific Study of Religion* 71 (1968): 23-40.

wave, they are confident that they will find the middle way between these extremes.

REVIVAL AND THE POLITICS OF THE KINGDOM

Though statements about "exported gospels" persist in the literature, Brazilian Pentecostalism is a collection of mostly indigenous movements that pick and choose from international charismatic and neo-Pentecostal sources.[43] The increasing self-supporting, self-governing and self-propagating nature of these movements effectively counters the argument that they are part of a Western funded conspiracy of the religious right. While the Brazilian *crentes* (believers, as most Protestants are called) I interviewed often spoke of the Brazilian genius of imitation and adaptation they, nonetheless, strongly disagreed with the idea that Brazilian Pentecostalism is "owned and operated" by foreign powers and influences.[44] I pointed out that in each of the three waves of twentieth century Brazilian Protestantism/Pentecostalism, the three dynamics of revival (the *indigenization* of leadership and organization, the *inculturation* of the gospel into local world view categories and the practical *contextualization* of Christian values through actions of justice and mercy) can be seen with increasing intensity.

How do revivals change their world? How does a movement shift from the experience of personal salvation to programs with the cultural dynamic of revival, that of social, political and economic contextualization? Pentecostal morality and strict personal discipline has helped to rebuild family life, challenge the destructive street ethic of *machismo* and renew neighborhoods. It builds social capital in the lives

---

[43]Note Peter Berger's helpful distinction that new movements of religious resurgence do not always choose the either-or of social and political rejection/marginalization or acceptance/conformity. The secularization thesis tended to see only these options. Berger argues that new religious movements often ignore secularization or respond to it with an ardent supernaturalism that moves beyond its restricted worldview. These new movements often opt for the third way of creative response that increases civil society and public space for the poor and marginalized. Cf. Peter Berger, ed., *The Desecularization of the World: Resurgent Religion and World Politics* (Grand Rapids: Eerdmans, 1999), p. 2.

[44]Rodriguiz/Montgomery, Vasvary and Vasvary interviews, March 5, 2006.

of men, women, families and civil society. But it has also been on the wrong side of many questions with its leaders falling to the temptations of power and prestige, and its movement often split by rivalry and competition.

Harvey Cox has argued that one of the most socially explosive aspects of Latin American Pentecostalism is its eschatology of "primal hope."[45] It is a vision of "Big Change" that shatters the pretensions of the status quo. Revival holds part of the answer to this question. Only in a state of revitalization and not routinization can Brazilian *crentes* see the reality of the kingdom in their midst and continue to question the status quo. The Brazilian Pentecost produced new light visionaries seeking the city of God where alternative societies and alternative visions of justice will help to challenge the economic and political orders. Religious and political elites eager to enjoy consensus and gain control of the process of change will be forced to make larger changes than before. When people's appetites are hungry for the kingdom of God then the usual business of conventional kingdoms simply will not satisfy.[46]

Rowan Ireland has argued "that the millions of Brazilian Pentecostals are acting politically, when they assert, celebrate and argue about their images of legitimate authority and righteousness and when they organize this *vida passageria* [life passage] for the Kingdom the Lord will bring."[47] We might wonder, however, how such primal hope works

---

[45]Harvey Cox, *Fire from Heaven: The Rise of Pentecostal Spirituality and the Reshaping of Religion in the Twenty-First Century* (Cambridge, Mass.: Da Capo Press, 1995), p. 82.

[46]Church and family provide the framework for morality and meaning and give a sense of the reality of the presence of the kingdom of God. "Persons, women as well as men, are individualized in a culturally novel way which carries a sense of unique worth and spiritually driven empowerment while at the same time grounding the individual in a network of mutual responsibilities and obligations" (Martin, *Pentecostalism*, p. 75). Kingdom of God consciousness thus has dramatic political and social consequences. One of the most dramatic has been the transformation of family life among the poor. Traditional slum life wreaked havoc on the family as the humiliated father descended into the "male prestige areas" of the bar, brothel, street, football stadium and drug culture. The new man created by charismatic conversion sees the arena of the family in new light. "Evangelicalism is a faith of the household poised against the seductions of the street" (Martin, *Pentecostalism*, 2002, p. 72).

[47]Rowan Ireland, *Kingdoms Come: Religion and Politics in Brazil* (Pittsburgh: University of Pittsburgh Press, 1992), quoted in Martin, *Pentecostalism*, 2002, p. 91.

practically to produce change? How does eschatology translate into effective contextualization of the gospel?

Jeff Haynes helps answer these questions. In his study of how new religious movements in both Christianity and Islam affect African politics he has used a Gramscian analysis but with a twist. In conventional Gramscian analysis the religious elite will often lobby the political elite for moderate reforms that will stabilize the political and social order and enable both elites to preserve position and power. Many Western style regimes prefer to rule by consensus rather than by coercion. Clerical elites rely on mass support by religious adherents in order to have leverage with political agents. Gramscian analysis suggests that this pacified populace, drugged on religion and circuses, are victims of a "false consciousness," selling the birthright of social justice for the porridge of moderate or even illusory reform.[48]

Herein lies the twist in Haynes's analysis. He shows how new religious movements, (many of which he would call fundamentalist) are often marginalized and criticized if they resist attempts to enlist them in the social and political agenda of the clerical elites. What both religious and political elites fear is popular change. The reason for this is obvious. It is harder to control. Popular religious or political movements can snowball. Their vision for change may go far beyond anything that moderate religious and political reformers propose. Revivalists, even if they are not overtly or conventionally political, may often prod political and religious elites to broaden their programs of change and embrace more dramatic reforms.[49] In Gram-

---

[48]For a summary of the Gramscian concept of hegemony and its application to power relations in modern nation-states cf. Roger Simon, *Gramsci's Political Thought: An Introduction* (London: Lawrence & Wishart, 1991), p. 22.

[49]Some scholars of "fundamentalist" movements talk about four models of movement-world relationship: "world rejecters" who give up on the dominant culture, "world creators" who form alternative societies (note that these two often go together), "world conquerors" (e.g., millennial movements, Islamists who seek to overthrow the dominant culture) and world transformers (who seek to reform the dominant culture through involvement in society and using civil society and persuasion to produce desired change). Pentecostalism in Brazil reflects aspects of

scian terms, the cluster of new Christian movements that make up such a large part of Brazilian Pentecostalism and Protestantism should be seen as an unfolding story of revitalized indigenous Christians experiencing and expressing the kingdom of God in surprising and varied ways.[50]

When Paulo Jr. and I arrived at the Goiânia Presbyterian Church on my last night in Brazil, I wasn't sure what to expect. Revival in Brazil had been a wild fire of growth, dynamism, division and broken relationships. Paulo Jr. was warmly received. The traditional Presbyterian Church that had expelled SDT decades before was now full of young people. The pastor publicly embraced Paulo Jr. as one of their own. Paulo Jr. and I shed a few tears at that reunion. It represented how revivals come of age. They emerge as protest movements during volatile times. They grow as movements of proclamation and conversion that verify their claims with healing and signs of deliverance. They move

all four models but is best placed in the world transformers category. See Gabriel Almond, R. Scott Appleby and Emmanuel Sivan, eds., *Strong Religion: The Rise of Fundamentalism Around the World* (Chicago: Unversity of Chicago Press, 2003), p. 148-49.
[50]Cf. Jeff Haynes, *Religion and Politics in Africa* (Nairobi: East African Educational Publishers, 1996). For primary readings on Gramsci cf. Antonio Gramsci, "The Antonio Gramsci Reader" <www.marxists.org/archive/gramsci/editions/reader/q07-19.htm>, accessed August 21, 2009. The pressure that popular Pentecostalism and its appeal to the poor put on Brazilian church leaders like Dom Helder Camara and the Brazilian Catholic establishment in the 1960s is a case in point. But how do popular movements and their call for big change help to produce a more just social, political and economic order? Rhetoric and vision is not enough. An insight from Michael Novak might help. One does not need to embrace Novak's democratic capitalism to appreciate the common sense that in a fallen world only institutions with limited power safeguard freedom and justice. The truisms that power corrupts and absolute power corrupts absolutely still make sense. Novak suggests that for democratic capitalism to work it requires the checks and balances of three interrelated systems: the political order, the economic order and the moral-cultural order. If capitalism captures the political system so that it passes laws that favor only the few or that compromises the moral-cultural order so that it gives silent consent to capitalism's savage tendencies, then inequities will increase. But what happens if there is sufficient pluralism within each of these three orders, alternative visions of justice and faith in the moral-cultural order; multiple voices heard and responded to in the political order; healthy and balanced competition in the economic order? Checks and balances both within and between these three orders could create the optimum soil for the seeds of new justice and a proliferation of empowerment even while it limits power monopolies in each of the three spheres. Revival Christianity may talk about the rule of the saints but it often unintentionally creates the conditions for the rule of sanity. Cf. Novak, *Spirit of Democratic Capitalism.*

their movement back into the world in mission to produce change that is line with the gospel and its promise of new heavens and new earth. After a season of resistance the old structures gradually embrace the new movement and the fires of revival diminish against the backdrop of an altered landscape. Just ask Paulo Jr.

8

NEW JERUSALEMS

Mensa Otabil, African Pentecostalism and Reverse Mission

On Christmas Day 2005 I attended the morning service of London's Kingsway International Christian Centre (KICC) which bills itself as the largest church in England. It claimed twelve thousand regular attendees in its many services and listed about ten daughter churches in Greater London as well as one in Nigeria. Situated in the Hackney section of London's East End, a favorite dumping ground for victims of gangland slayings, KICC occupies a 9.5 acre site in an industrial area. The location of the main service was in an enormous permanent "tent" that probably sat seven to eight thousand. After an opening thirty minutes of Vineyard-style worship, three Christmas presentations were offered to the congregation of about six thousand. The children gave a fairly conventional Christmas pageant. The young professionals did a jazz Christmas number with choreography. Finally, the West Indians did a calypso Christmas number complete with Limbo. These three presentations reflected KICC's core constituency: Young African families, West Indians and young African professionals.

After ninety minutes of music and drama I was expecting the benediction. Instead the founding pastor, Rev. Matthew Ashimolowo came on to the platform for his sermon. For another ninety minutes Ashimolowo offered a Pentecostal theology of hope that explained to a large degree why KICC has been so successful. Ashimolowo was dressed in traditional Nigerian garb. He preached on Luke 1 and the miracle of Christmas. His two strongly developed themes were that Christ is the first miracle of Christmas but that we as Christians being transformed by Christ are the second miracle of Christmas. Christ definitely received top billing. Noting the verse in Luke 1 in which "nothing is impossible with God," Ashimolowo developed a Christmas Christology based on the seven wonders of Jesus Christ.

Halfway through his preaching, Ashimolowo was still warming to his overall theme—how we, as Christians, are part of the miracle of Christmas. Christ was the cornerstone which the builders rejected so that we, the rejected ones, could become the new building of God in spite of our rejection—a message received with a roar of approval. "There is a lifter who will lift you up," he dramatically announces to more applause. "He makes miracles out of the ridiculous. . . . Just as on the night of Christ's birth there was no miscarriage so with our dreams for 2006 there will be no miscarriage. God will do his new miracle. Satan may do everything he can to frustrate those dreams but just like at Christmas God will do the impossible and bring the miracle to pass." It was a Christmas message like few I have heard before.

How does a Nigerian ex-Muslim plant a church of twelve thousand in the heart of secular England? There are many factors that go into such a phenomenon not the least of which are the work of the Holy Spirit and the providence of God, factors that lie beyond the scrutiny of a historian. But like many other faces of World Christianity global revivals act as the delivery system for most of these dynamics of growth and expansion. This certainly seems true in Africa.

NEO-PENTECOSTALISM

If the Aladura movement can be seen as a religious revival as we have argued in previous pages, then neo-Pentecostalism must be seen as a revival *extraordinaire*.[1] The emergence of these new churches since the late 1970s has been explosive. "In any major African city, form Harare to Freetown, from Nairobi to Kinshasa, these new churches were to be found every Sunday in schoolrooms, cinemas, theatres, halls and hotel conference rooms."[2] Not only are these churches everywhere but they are also new arrivals on the African religious landscape.

"Idahosa's Church of God International in Nigeria, Otabil's International Central Gospel Church in Accra, Wutawanashe's Family of God in Zimbabwe, Leslie's Abundant Life in Kampala, Gitonga's Redeemed Gospel Church in Kenya, are now huge churches that simply did not exist twenty, in some cases even ten, years ago." These new charismatic churches were built on the foundation of older Pentecostal churches that joined with the more innovative new churches to fuel the tides of religious change in Africa.[3]

Paul Gifford notes that the growth of these new churches has been at the expense of many of the mainline churches. Mainline churches in Africa have lost some of their appeal due to an over identification with corrupt regimes eager for church support, abuses of power by church leadership and a process of NGO-ization whereby the spiritual needs of people were neglected due to an over attention on social and economic development. So alarmed were the mainline churches at the erosion of their membership by Pentecostals that the All Africa Conference of Churches (AACC) initiated a project in the late 1980s to investigate the trend and help member churches respond.[4] Mainline churches were concerned over the lack of social and political en-

---

[1]Cf. Alan Anderson. *An Introduction to Pentecostalism* (Cambridge: Cambridge University Press, 2004); Harvey Cox, *Fire from Heaven: The Rise of Pentecostal Spirituality and the Reshaping of Religion in the Twenty-first Century* (London: Cassell, 1996); and Philip Jenkins, *The Next Christendom: The Coming of Global Christianity* (New York: Oxford University Press, 2002). Jenkins: "To use the language of revivalism, Africa has now for over a century been engaged in a continuous encounter with Pentecostal fires" (p. 51).

[2]Paul Gifford, "Some Recent Developments in African Christianity," *African Affairs* 93, no. 373 (October 1994): 514-15.

[3]Ibid.

[4]Ibid., pp. 520-21.

gagement and reform, not to mention how the new churches were taking their sheep.

The character and cultural implications of the neo-Pentecostal revival in Africa become clearer when viewed as an instance of global revival. I would like to focus on one of the more prominent "new light" leaders of African neo-Pentecostalism, Mensa Otabil, founder of the International Central Gospel Church (ICGC) and chancellor of Central University College, a respected private university in Ghana. While the ICGC has branches in different part of Africa and Europe, it is by no means at the cutting edge of reverse mission. That honor would have to go to the Redeemed Christian Church of God with branches in one hundred ten countries. Why then focus on Ghana and Otabil? His missional credentials are impressive enough. As one researcher states: "The church has launched more than a hundred satellites including two congregations in the United States, and one each in England, the Netherlands and South Africa. The 'Living Word' television program is broadcast in Kenya, and South Africa. In Pentecostal conferences that affirm each other's ministries and messages Otabil is a frequent preacher."[5] But that is not the main reason for featuring Otabil. His story helps explain the roots of reverse mission, whereby Africa is now sending missionaries to the West. At the center of this reverse mission is a dynamic missional paradigm fueling the current third wave of global Pentecostal expansion.

MENSA OTABIL, THE ICGC AND THE GLOBAL MISSION OF GOD

Neo-Pentecostalism in Africa generally and in the life of Mensa Otabil in particular needs to be seen against the West African backdrop of both widespread disillusionment with nationalism and fervent revivalism. The story of disillusionment is well known. The new nations of Africa had promised much. Ghana's leader at independence, Kwame

---

[5]A. Christian van Gorder, "Beyond the Rivers of Africa: The Afrocentric Pentecostalism of Mensa Otabil," *Pneuma* 30 (2008): 34.

Nkrumah, captured the aspirations of his generation in 1962: "We'll transform the Gold Coast [Ghana] into a paradise in ten years."[6] On his statue in Accra, Nkrumah has inscribed the words, "Seek first the political kingdom and all things will be added unto you." When Nkrumah's corrupt and authoritarian regime collapsed in 1966, a bleak era of political centralization and economic decline lay ahead. Gifford summarizes this decline: "The background in black Africa was increasing social, political and economic collapse." On almost every front African nations lost ground in the 1980s. According to UN sources "the African was generally 40 per cent worse off in 1991 than in 1980. . . . The continent was slipping out of the Third World and into its own bleak category of Nth world."[7] Nkrumah's paradise had not materialized and the almost religious reverence for nationalism epitomized by Nkrumah himself and shared widely across the continent turned into disillusionment and a search for alternatives.[8]

One of those alternatives became Pentecostalism. The youth revival that swept through Nigeria during the civil war (1967-1970) and its immediate aftermath reshaped the religious landscape of Nigeria and Ghana. Ogbu Kalu has argued that this revival was important in changing the Christian paradigm of Nigeria from a missionary Christianity to "a deep religious structure that undergirds all the varieties of African traditional religion, a religion with power."[9] This revival acted as a bridge between the older missionary Christianity and the neo-Pentecostal movement of the 1980s.

The branches of the youth revival were several. Major components of this revival included: the hour of redemption ministry; Benson Idahosa's evangelistic ministry; Scripture Union; *Hour of Freedom* minis-

---

[6]Kwame Nkrumah in *I Speak of Freedom* (Oxford, 1962), quoted in Crawford Young, "The End of the Post-Colonial State in Africa?" *African Affairs* 103, no. 410 (2004): 30.

[7]Gifford, "Some Recent Developments in African Christianity," p. 513.

[8]The despair of Ghana's failed nationalism is eloquently chronicled in Ayi Kwei Armah, *The Beautiful Ones Are Not Yet Born* (London: Heinemann, 1988).

[9]Ogbu Kalu, "Passive Revolution and Its Saboteurs: African Christian Initiative in the Era of Decolonization, 1955-1975," in *Missions, Nationalism and the End of Empire*, ed. Brian Stanley and Alaine Low (Grand Rapids: Eerdmans, 2003), p. 270.

try; Christian unions; and, finally, the charismatic impact of the National Youth Service Corp.[10]

Many youth were troubled by the political volatility of Nigeria in the
sixties when religious, political and ethnic factionalism kept the nation on
the brink. Scripture Union (SU) attracted a generation of students looking for permanence and stability and began to both disciple and mobilize
them for mission. Started in Britain in 1950s, Scripture Union emphasized inductive Bible study, prayer and discipleship groups in schools.
When Nigerian schools were closed in 1967 at the outbreak of civil war,
SU underwent profound change. New traveling secretary, Bill Roberts,
decided to stay on despite the war. A Bible study he led was visited with
special power resulting in "deep conversion, deliverance, evangelism and
relief work."[11] This local revival "spread like wild fire as young people
formed prayer and evangelistic bands in their village." The conditions of
the war drove many to the prayer fellowships of Scripture Union. From
the ranks of these discipled and mobilized youth would come "new light
leaders" who would amplify the revival throughout the region.

Benson Idahosa is a case in point. After coming back from Bible
school in Dallas, Texas, Idahosa formed the Church of God mission.
"By 1970 his theology was developing some themes from T. L. Os-
born's teaching" on prosperity.[12] For those coming out of the devastation of civil war, this new paradigm had power. Soon Idahosa was the
head of a multifaceted ministry involving a "huge miracle center, television ministry, All Nations for Christ Bible school, and the effective
musical group called Redemption Voices."[13]

Bill Roberts also played a key role in the conversion of three young
men—Stephen Okafor, Raphael Okaphor and Arthur Orizu. Influenced by new age literature in their quest for spiritual light and power,
they had wandered through the Aladura churches as well. They formed

---

[10]Ogbu Kalu, ed., *African Christianity: An African Story* (Trenton/Asmara: Africa World Press,
2007), pp. 264-65.
[11]Ibid., p. 301.
[12]Kalu, "Passive Revolution and Its Saboteurs," p. 273.
[13]Ibid.

The Hour of Freedom Evangelistic Association and were key agents of revival and mass conversion in Igboland between 1970 and 1971. They also helped renew SU branches in many of the schools, some of which became charismatic.

The civil war affected the religious landscape in several ways. New occult groups flourished. African Initiated Churches (AICs) were in transition. The Aladura churches underwent renewal. Yet another stream that fed West African revivalism began in 1962 when the local Christian Union (CU—a campus ministry in higher education) broke away from the SCM (Student Christian Movement) over theological issues. They organized prayer meetings and preaching crusades at universities and schools. The charismatic model of Christianity was widely spread through the CU. Steady voices like G. Elton (a mentor of Idahosa) helped minimize the spiritual rivalry from different charismatic groups, bringing many of them under the united front of Grace of God mission. By 1973 a new wing of the movement, Christian Youth Corpers, gave the CU new evangelistic power and scope.

How did this youth revival spread to the rest of Nigeria and beyond? Newly saved young people from these various ministries joined the mandatory National Youth Service Corp. As Christian members were assigned to different parts of the country they helped spread the new message of salvation and power in the Spirit to those who accept Jesus as Savior and Lord.

These various strands were the tip of Pentecostal renewal worldwide. The third wave movement, as labeled by Peter Wagner and which had John Wimber and the Vineyard movement as one of its pioneers, spread through much of English-speaking Africa. It combined the Reformation and evangelical message of the cross and personal salvation with the new emphasis on spiritual power through the Holy Spirit that paved the way for a rich cascade of neo-Pentecostalism. This wave of West African revival washed over the shores of Ghana and a dozen African countries.

The impact of the youth revival in Nigeria on Ghana was profound.

As Kalu writes: "By the late 1980s a number of Pentecostal ministries in Ghana started vigorous missionary activities along the Atlantic coast. The Ghana Evangelical Missionary Association Christian Outreach Foundation (1987), African Christian Missions (1984) and Torchbearers (1987) are only a few."[14] When Nigerian evangelist Benson Idahosa visited Accra in 1978, one of the converts he left behind was Christy Doe Teteh, who became dissatisfied in her Roman Catholic Church and began the quest for deeper life. In 1989 she formed Solid Rock Chapel in Accra, a church of several thousand known for its deliverance ministries and its prayer band, the Striking Force.

The impact of neo-Pentecostal revivalism in Ghana in the 1980s was documented by a careful research conducted by the Ghana Evangelism Committee in 1986-1987. Traditional AICs like the Musama Disco Christo Church and the Church of the Twelve Apostles declined by an average of 20 percent. Though the mainline churches (Anglican, Presbyterian and Methodist) held their own or grew modestly the real growth was with churches connected to the revival. Groups such as the Apostolic Church, the Church of Pentecost and the Assemblies of God mushroomed significantly. By the mid-1980s the Western African charismatic awakening was well into moving out of the problem stage of leadership clashes and into the paradigm stage of defining its message and consolidating its converts.[15]

Otabil's story begins at this busy intersection of state decline and charismatic resurgence. Born in 1960 Otabil grew up in Ghana's decade of despair. Raised on the outskirts of Accra, his father died when Otabil was six. This tragedy devastated the family emotionally and financially.[16] Despite his family's extreme poverty, Otabil was able to

[14]Ogbu Kalu, *African Pentecostalism: An Introduction* (Oxford: Oxford University Press, 2008), p. 152.
[15]Gifford, "Some Recent Developments in African Christianity," pp. 513-15.
[16]E. Kingsley Larbi, "The Development of Ghanaian Pentecostalism: A Study in the Appropriation of the Christian Gospel in Twentieth Century Ghana Setting with Special Reference to the Christ Apostolic Church, the Church of Pentecost, and the International Central Gospel Church" (Ph.D. diss., University of Edinburgh, 1995), p. 300.

finish secondary school. Like some of the Aladura leaders mentioned earlier, he grew up in the Anglican church but shifted to a Pentecostal church, Temu Fellowship, after his evangelical conversion at age twelve. After high school, Otabil found employment with the Information Services department as a technical officer.

His real love, however, was pursuing the Spirit. His restless search for deeper spiritual experience led Otabil to the Power House Fellowship where he experienced the baptism of the Spirit in 1975. In 1976 Otabil moved to the Kanda section of Accra. By 1981 he became head of the Kanda Christian Fellowship. After Lt. J. J. Rawlings and his Armed Forces Revolutionary Council (AFRC) seized power during his second coup attempt in 1981 (called "The Second Coming"), Otabil identified with the aspirations of the new movement and became president of the Kanda Peoples Defense Committee, a civilian chapter of the AFRC.[17]

The rise of a new light leader begins the personal translation of biblical truth into vernacular categories and worldview. For Otabil this translation process took place over five years of reflection between 1982 to 1986. The initial elements of his new paradigm were pieced together from American Kenneth Hagan's prosperity gospel, Ghanaian Duncan Williams local adaptations of that theme and his ministry involvement at Kanda Fellowship. By early 1983 his spiritual restlessness resurfaced. He declared his intention to create a new church. In 1984 he founded the International Central Gospel Church.[18]

The years 1985 through 1989 were critical in clarifying his new light. By 1986 Otabil publically declared that the older churches were "Babylon" led by "vipers" and "unconverted ministers."[19] He called for true Christians to leave such churches and move to where the Spirit was at work. At the same time as his radical break with the Protestant mainstream in Ghana he distanced himself from North American teachers of the faith or prosperity gospel. As an alternative to main-

---

[17]Ibid., p. 301.
[18]Ibid., p. 302.
[19]Ibid., p. 313.

stream African Christianity and imported American Pentecostalism, Otabil began to form a Pentecostal biblical theology of liberation and reconstruction heavily influenced by the themes of African selfhood associated with the negritude movement of Leopold Senghor and Abdou Diouf and that found in Scripture. [20] He dropped his Christian name, David. Otabil began to clarify a vision of the church that would "lift up the image of the black man so that he can be a channel of blessing to all men."

It is here that Otabil's Afrocentric gospel begins. In his sermons and in his book *Beyond the Rivers of Ethiopia*[21] Otabil investigates the "mental slavery" that still imprisons the African soul. He speaks of "bondage in freedom" by which he means that Africa, despite political independence, is still shackled to psychological and spiritual bondage that is slavery's legacy. Slavery and colonialism constructed an African self-image that many in the church have internalized. The good is associated with the colonial culture and the bad becomes the local and homegrown. "Many black people," Otabil writes, "have mentally accepted the logic of black as inferior." Such an idea is crippling for the realization of African Christianity's potential.[22] He rejects the idea that the "church in Africa should be ruled from anywhere but Africa" and "our finances must be generated from the productive work of our own resources." Otabil is clearly moving beyond the health and wealth gospel of miraculous receiving and pushes toward a re-envisioned Protestant work ethic.[23]

Critical to his theology is the use of biblical history to produce a positive fatalism that empowers African Christians to engage in the mission of God without fear of failure. To foster this positive theology Otabil walks through the Bible, demonstrating how God used black men throughout the history of redemption. Beginning with the Cush-

---

[20]Ibid., p. 302.
[21]Mensa Otabil, *Beyond the Rivers of Ethiopa: A Biblical Revelation on God's Purpose for the Black Race* (Accra, Ghana: Altar International, 1992).
[22]Ibid., p. 71.
[23]Ibid., p. 68.

ites, Jethro, Midianites and Zephaniah, Otabil moves to New Testament figures such as the Ethiopian eunuch, Simon of Niger and Lucius. God used these black men to prepare for and spread the gospel of liberation through Christ.[24] Building on this biblical history he returns to the first chapter of Genesis (1:28) and the four laws of productivity that will lift the African from material bondage: being fruitful (creating), multiplying (expanding and distributing what we create), filling the earth (culture building) and subduing (managing success in growth in a godly way). God's destiny is for the black race to once again play a key role in bringing the blessings of God to all men through the transformation of black men and women through the gospel of grace and the laws of productivity.[25]

Abraham is a key for Otabil. The way to restore a vision for God's purpose for Africa is to return to the call of Abraham. Just as Abram turned his back on the old nation of Ur to become a new nation, the implication is that God is doing a similar thing in our day with the shift from global North to global South. "The old nation was reprobate but the new nation would be approved and accepted of God." Additionally, while "the Old Nation built its own kingdom, the new [nation] would build God's kingdom and establish his rule and policies on the face of the earth."[26] Hampering the African response to God's call to transform the world through the gospel is the problem of dependency. "How can an individual be a blessing when he is always receiving and never giving?" Otabil asks.

What light does this paradigm shed on how revivals engage in global missions? How does this vision help explain African missionary expansion in Africa and Europe? Otabil points to eschatology as the basis of African missions. Van Gorder summarizes: "Since they have been endowed with the true way, African Pentecostals must 'turn around and

---

[24]E. Kingsley Larbi, *Pentecostalism: The Eddies of Ghanian Christianity* (Accra, Ghana: Centre for Pentecostal and Charismatic Studies, 2001), pp. 349-52.
[25]Ibid., pp. 353-56.
[26]Otabil, *Beyond the Rivers of Ethiopia*, p. 23.

see what God is doing' in the world today. Otabil believes that 'the total liberation of black people will be preceded by a major revival of God's power and glory in the nations.'"[27]

Revivals, if they are to succeed and propel a movement outward, must raise up indigenous leaders, formulate a powerful biblical message that speaks deeply to the context and organize their followers into missional structures that will carry out the vision. By 1989 Otabil had accomplished these tasks. But an additional task remained. In the power stage of a revival, successful conflict resolution with resistant powers often precedes the dynamic expansion of the group into new areas and issues. Otabil had to deal with some burned bridges. The organizing of the ICGC severely strained relations with both mainline and classic Pentecostal churches, groups that he condemned as "vipers."[28]

During the 1990s Otabil took up the task of mending these broken relations with other groups. His rapprochement led to a wider diffusion of his movement. His positive and constructive biblical theology became a paradigm against which others were measured. Paul Gifford talks about the "Otabilization" of Ghanaian neo-Pentocostalism claiming that other leading neo-Pentecostal preachers are picking up the themes of good governance, hard work and breaking the dependency on the West.[29] Ogbu Kalu has called Otabil's biblical vision an "Evangelical-Pentecostal Liberation Theology."[30] Gifford feels that Otabil is moving beyond liberation to a more positive theology of reconstruction.[31]

Otabil may well be the most impressive example of the new light leaders emerging from Ghanaian neo-Pentecostalism but he identifies with his mentors and colleagues in the prosperity movement and they

---

[27]Van Gorder, "Beyond the Rivers of Africa," pp. 33-34.
[28]Larbi, "Development of Ghanian Pentecostalism," p. 313.
[29]Paul Gifford, *Ghana's New Christianity* (Bloomington: Indiana University Press, 2004), p. 198.
[30]Ogbu Kalu quoted in Larbi, *Pentecostalism*, p. 1.
[31]Gifford, *Ghana's New Christianity*, p. 135.

in turn are increasingly influenced by his leadership.[32] The neo-Pentecostal revival is advancing into the power stage where new structures, new status and even new systems will be shaped by the movement. One of the expressions of this third stage is new mission, a mission that is spilling out beyond places of origin and following global cultural highways around the world in reverse mission. African churches can now be found in major cities not only across Africa, but also North America, Britain and the European continent. The Redeemed Christian Church of God (RCCG) under the leadership of E. A. Adeboye

---

[32]Gifford's scholarship on the new Pentecostalism in Africa seems to have grown in two distinct ways over a nearly decade and a half of insightful articles and books. He has broadened his understanding of the vagaries of a brand of Christianity with which he clearly does not identify while at the same time deepening his questioning of neo-Pentecostalism's actual influence on social and political life. He seems more skeptical of the social value of neo-Pentecostalism in *Ghana's New Christianity* than in his earlier work. He wrote in 1994 that this "new community provides free social space." Millions of Africa members "find shelter, psychological security, solidarity." These Christian communities "create a new world, a new existence for themselves, away from the harsh and brutalizing realities of their former existence." Here "in this new world they can forge a new notion of the self, for here they can begin to make personal decisions. . . . They interact as equals." As members of this new community "they learn patterns of discipline and independence" (Paul Gifford, "Ghana's Charismatic Churches," *Journal of Religion in Africa* [1994]: 241-65). Not to be overlooked is the contribution that these new churches are making to civil society (the network of nongovernmental voluntary groups that work toward public goals and ends). Civil society is regarded as crucial for democratization—the process of dissent and debate within the boundaries of civility that moves a nation forward. "From this perspective, it is obvious why churches have become so important to Africa's democratization," writes Gifford. "In so many one-party states, the churches became the greatest single element of civil society" (Gifford, "Ghana's Charismatic Churches," pp. 20-22). Writing in 1994 on the neo-Pentecostal churches in Liberia, Gifford gave three additional reasons for the appeal of neo-Pentecostal churches, reasons which seem to apply to Ghana as well. First was the certainty they offer in the confusing world of Liberia by their stress on the Bible and its authority. "Second, to join these churches was to move into an alternative society. Belonging to these churches was not a Sunday morning activity, which Christianity was for most of Liberia's nominal mainline Christians. . . . As social support systems collapsed, the importance of entering a new family cannot be overemphasized." Third, the churches addressed the whole of life. They each offered courses on marriage, friendship, and provided a clinic certain days of the week (see Paul Gifford, ed., *New Dimensions in African Christianity* [Nairobi: All Africa Conference of Churches, 1992] and Gifford, "Some Recent Developments in African Christianity," pp. 531-33). A kind of Christianity that remaps the mazeway of culture in ways that reshapes time and space, promotes civil society, builds social capital, provides an alternative polis and new social networks as strong as family and addresses the whole of life are culturally transformative churches. They are forces of cultural revitalization. They are politically and socially relevant in ways that transcend the easy categories of global capitalism or conventional politics.

has expanded rapidly in its native Nigeria, claiming fourteen thousand branches in that nation alone. More remarkably the RCCD has churches, as mentioned above, in one hundred ten countries and has sent missionaries to resistant nations like China, Pakistan and Malaysia.[33] African Christian revivalism helps to explain this energy, vision and sheer size of African Christianity expansion in the last twenty-five years.[34] African churches like the RCCD are clear indicators that the religious expansion of the twenty-first century, unlike the nineteenth, is no longer from "the West to the rest" but increasingly "from everywhere to everywhere." African Christian expansion to Europe has initiated what Gerrie ter Haar has called "a new chapter in European Christian History."[35]

MAKING SENSE OF NEO-PENTECOSTALISM IN AFRICA

Ogbu Kalu, the late Nigerian historian of African Christianity, has helped me understand the power of indigenous movements in Africa. Kalu recognizes that not everyone sees much that is positive coming out of the neo-Pentecostal movement. He recaps some of the most common criticisms of the new African Christianity whose exaggerated supernaturalism "obscures rationality, ignores democratic values, and fails to mobilize social capital."[36]

Kalu rejects the scholarship of Afro-pessimism and calls for a new model, championed by a number of indigenous scholars "labeled African Renaissance or Afro-optimism."[37] This latter view moves beyond the discourse of modernity and calls for an appreciation of "covert" politics, the problem of magic in African political life, the great variety of political

---

[33]Lisa Miller, "E. A. Adeboye," *Newsweek,* January 5, 2009 <www.newsweek.com/id/176333>.
[34]For an expert overview of the expansion of African Christianity into Europe and North America see Afe Adogame, "African Christian Communities in Diaspora," in Ogbu Kalu, *African Christianity: An African Story* (Pretoria: University of Pretoria, 2005), pp. 494-519.
[35]Gerrie ter Haar, *Halfway to Paradise: African Christians in Europe* (Cardiff: Cardiff Academic Press, 1998).
[36]Kalu, *African Pentecostalism*, p. 194.
[37]Ibid., p. 196.

responses by Pentecostal groups across Africa and finally, the role that "sacralization" of the political order plays in modern nation building.[38]

As agents of a religious renaissance in Africa, neo-Pentecostalism has gained confidence to export an Africanized gospel to the African enclaves of urban centers in Europe and beyond. As Alan Anderson explains:

> Pentecostals in Africa proclaim a pragmatic gospel that seeks to address practical needs like sickness, poverty, unemployment, loneliness, evil spirits and sorcery. In varying degrees and in their many and varied forms, and precisely because of their inherent flexibility, these Pentecostals attain an authentically indigenous character which enables them to offer answers to some of the fundamental questions asked in their own context. A sympathetic approach to local culture and the retention of certain cultural practices are undoubtedly major reasons for their attraction, especially for those millions overwhelmed by urbanization with its transition from a personal rural society to an impersonal urban one. At the same time, Pentecostals confront old views by declaring what they are convinced is a more powerful protection against sorcery and a more effective healing from sickness than either the existing churches or the traditional rituals had offered. Healing, guidance, protection from evil, and success and prosperity are some of the practical benefits offered to faithful members of Pentecostal churches.[39]

For large numbers of Africans both inside and outside Africa, those practical benefits are not only pragmatic reasons to affiliate but signs that the kingdom of God has broken into history and has changed them and their world forever.

THE CITY OF GOD INSIDE THE CITY OF MAN

Revived churches are missional churches and the new churches of Asia, Africa and Latin America are moving beyond local and national con-

---

[38]Ibid., p. 200.
[39]Alan Anderson, "Evangelism and the Growth of Pentecostalism in Africa," <http://artsweb .bham.ac.uk/aanderson/> then click "Online Papers" then click "Evangelism and the Growth of Pentecostalism in Africa."

texts to embrace the global context. Many of these revival movements have created new movements of reverse mission, sending missionaries to the lands that formerly sent missionaries to them. This reverse mission, born of revival, is making a strong impact in places like London, Berlin, New York and Kiev to name but a few locales. The AICs of Africa, neo-Pentecostal movements of Brazil and Africa, Asian movements from South Korea and the Chinese Diaspora are seeking to make an impact in the Western world challenging the adjective "post-Christian" as it is often used of the North Atlantic community.[40]

Global revivals produce reverse mission. Immigration may establish a presence but only indigenous movements that seek to change their world using the resources of classic Christianity can turn presence into a paradigm shift. When neo-Pentecostalism is viewed through the lens of global revivalism we can get a greater understanding of its inherently missional and crosscultural dynamism. The revival paradigm produces an "optimistic fatalism" so desperately needed by an immigrant community struggling for survival and identity. If God is for me, who then can be against me. The power of this thinking is couched in the language of prosperity and material gain. But these are but symbols of the power of God to control the world of matter and for many extend the lordship of Christ over, not just the spiritual and relationship issues of life, but also everyday issues of urban life and survival. In Augustine's famous reading of history as the struggle between the city of God and the city of man, revivals empower individuals to see their personal struggles in such cosmic terms, and more importantly see their fight as one that God fights for them as well as with them.

After the Christmas service in London, I interviewed several people at KICC to find out how they got involved and what kept them coming back for more. Joyce is a Kenyan who came to UK for further studies and had married and settled down in London. She became a Christian

---

[40]Adogame, "African Christian Communities in Diaspora," p. 204. See also Jehu Hanciles, *Beyond Christendom: Globalization, African Migration, and the Transformation of the West* (Maryknoll, N.Y.: Orbis, 2008).

back in Nairobi during high school days and took her active faith with her to England. She had trouble finding a church that felt like home but eventually started attending KICC in the mid-1990s. She expressed concern about the growth of the church and the loss of intimacy. When she started coming there were several hundred and it felt like family. With the rapid expansion to twelve thousand that intimacy had been lost. She admitted that the church did offer prayer groups to foster community on a more human scale, but she had not become involved even though she had offered to host one of these groups in her home. She had not heard from the church. What kept her coming back I asked? "I love the preaching," said Joyce. "Pastor Matthew's sermons are so relevant. I would have trouble finding that elsewhere."

Her husband Glenn had different reasons for coming. Glen is a second-generation British-Jamaican who had recently renewed his faith through the church and the influence of his wife. He had given up church as did his nominally Anglican family when he was in his teens. His father's serious health issues helped to draw him back to Christianity, particularly one which promised miracles. He got a lot out of the preaching and felt that God gave him something each week that was just for him.

Aris was a young professional in the British film industry from Nigerian background but born in UK. Her mother's dramatic change from practicing traditional religion a few years ago after coming to KICC helped to attract her. She accepted Christ not long after coming and was involved in one of the numerous ministry teams that fed the homeless in London.

Each of three participants was educated, articulate and employed. They did not fit the profile of the disenfranchised in typical ways although each belonged to a minority community within the UK. KICC made the presence of God in Christ real and vivid and equipped them to embrace God as an exchange partner who was willing and able to help them with the material and existential issues of life. Such revival paradigms produce compelling missional practice. Through missional practice they begin to change the world.

9

TAMING THE DRAGON

Zhang Rongliang and the Chinese House Churches

On the night of August 22, 1998, near the city of Zhengxhou, Henan's provincial capital, a secret meeting of Chinese house church leaders took place. Representatives of four of the major house church networks had gathered to conclude two years of quiet negotiations between the groups.[1] One of the organizers, Zhang Rongliang, a senior leader of the Fangcheng fellowship, one of China's largest house churches (estimated at ten million), had come to this unity meeting along a tortuous path.

The house churches had been divided for nearly two decades, partly over competition for foreign partners and dollars, partly over doctrinal disagreements but mostly due to personal slights and jealousies. Zhang bore his share of personal slights. He reportedly cycled a great distance

---

[1]The house church networks represented were Fangcheng, Tanghe, Born Again and Anhui. It is important to note that by 2002 the Born Again movement had been excluded from the network. The Shouters (Local Church) though not represented at the 1998 meetings have also been excluded on doctrinal grounds despite charitable statements contained in the three documents of 1998. Cf. David Aikman, *Jesus in Beijing: How Christianity Is Transforming China and Changing the Global Balance of Power* (Washington, D.C.: Regnery, 2003), pp. 93-94. Aikman includes the three documents of 1998 including the "United Appeal" in two appendices in his book. Little will be said about Aikman's overall narrative in this essay which is heavily slanted in favor of the house churches of China and against the Three Self Patriotic churches.

to hear another house church leader, Brother Xu, head of the Born Again house churches. After he arrived, Xu's handlers barred Zhang from any audience with their leader. Zhang was deeply embittered by this and gave up on seeking reconciliation for many years.

Others were more persistent. Brother Yun wrote in his autobiography, *The Heavenly Man*, that after a vision from the Lord to seek unity among the house fellowships he found Zhang whom he had worked with for many years. Zhang's response to the idea of house church unity, according to Yun, was a hearty laugh. "That's impossible! The different groups you want to bring together are typical cults. We'll have nothing to do with them."[2] Yun arranged a meeting between Zhang and Xu. There was deep repentance on both sides and agreement to work together "wherever possible."

In November of 1996 leaders of the five largest house church networks met together in Shanghai, with Zhang among them. After agreeing to work together and learn from one another "all the leaders took communion together." Yun speculates that it was the "first time in more than 50 years that the top leaders of China's church had taken the Lord's Supper in unity."[3]

Given the decades of struggle for unity, Zhang must have smiled on that August 1998 night as they put the finishing touches on a handwritten document entitled "A United Appeal of the Various Branches of the Chinese House Church" (hereafter the "United Appeal"). The seven numbered paragraphs requested the government of China to "release unconditionally all House Church Christians" imprisoned in the vast gulag of "Labor Reform Camps."[4] Paragraph three claimed that since there were eighty million believers in the house churches as opposed to only ten million in the government-sanctioned Three Self Church (or Three Self Patriotic Movement, TSPM) it was time for the

---

[2]Paul Hathaway, Zhenying Liu and Brother Yun, *The Heavenly Man* (Grand Rapids: Kregel, 2003), p. 235.
[3]Ibid., p. 240.
[4]"A United Appeal of the Various Branches of the Chinese House Church," in Aikman, *Jesus in Beijing*, p. 293.

government to admit that "the House Church represents the main stream of Christianity in China." The TSPM could no more represent Christianity, declared the Appeal, than Taiwan could represent China. Paragraph three went on to accuse the official church of "serious deviation" in "many spiritual matters." The Appeal, representing a significant percentage of the claimed eighty million members of the unregistered churches, concluded that since the "Chinese House Church is the channel through which God's blessings come to China" the government's persecution "has blocked this channel of blessing."

Zhang gave the unsigned document to two invited Western journalists, Mark O'Keefe of the *Oregonian* and David Aikman of *Time*, with the request that they publicize this document in the Western press. Over the next several months additional meetings were held and two other important documents were drafted, the "Confession of Faith of House Churches in China" (hereafter the "Confession") and the "Attitude of Chinese House Churches toward the Government, Its Religious Policy and the Three Self Movement" (hereafter the "Attitude"). Taken together, the three apologetic documents of 1998 marked an important moment in the house churches' attempt to resolve its ongoing conflict with the Chinese state.

I heard about this important unity movement on a trip to China a few years after Zhang and his brothers had gathered on that hot August night. I heard more about the ongoing conflict between house churches and registered churches. On an overnight stay in Hong Kong I learned more about the "United Appeal," "Confession" and "Attitude" documents. When I returned home I made a point to find these documents and study them more carefully. Why would a movement born out of decades of revival need these documents? What were they trying to accomplish? How effective was the "United Appeal" in placating government wrath? How historically Christian was the "Confession?" How useful was the "Attitude"?

Slowly the picture began to emerge of a revival movement in its last stage of development—the power phase. The opening challenge of the power stage, however, is apologetics—an attempt to answer critics and resolve conflict. If a movement resolves key areas of conflict internally and externally, it frequently moves on to the climax of the power stage—expansion and impact on the surrounding culture. What follows is my take on how revivals manage that all-important final challenge of conflict resolution in the unleashing of a movement.

My hunch? Seen from the perspective of global revivals, the documents of 1998 are less an attempt to stop government persecution and more a strategy to optimize conditions for continued growth by increasing their popular appeal.[5] In a twenty-first century China still shaped by Deng Xiaoping's slogan "Seek Truth from Facts," size may be the best apologetic.

"Canny About Conflict"—Revivals and Conflict Resolution

I began my search for answers by going back to Anthony Wallace's classic study of renewal movements (or revitalization movements in his parlance). Wallace suggested that in the final stages of a people movement, as it begins to impact the wider world, conflict increases both internally and externally. Left unresolved this conflict may reach crisis proportions. If the movement is able to handle the conflict successfully it grows in numbers and in influence. If it doesn't the movement contracts and eventually declines and dies.

I could think of a number of revival movements in history that were unable to resolve conflict enough to make it through that power stage. Why did some movements succeed at conflict resolution and others fail? Wallace had two answers and both dealt with realism as a factor. First, a movement needs to be realistic about goals. This goes back to the movement's gospel message. While global revivals are almost by definition unrealistic as they envision new worlds being born, successful

---

[5]Cf. the discussion of the effectiveness of "acephalous" church and parachurch structures in the worldwide spread of Pentecostalism in Luther Gerlach and Virginia Hine, "Five Factors Crucial to the Growth and Spread of a Modern Religious Movement," *Journal for the Scientific Study of Religion* 7, no. 1 (1968): 23-40.

movements are realistic about the degree of change that the movement can expect in any given moment in history. Theologians talk about the "already" and "not yet" aspects of the kingdom of God. Christians live in the tension between what has already come by way of kingdom benefits (new life in Christ, healing, prosperity, charismatic community, future hope, a mission in this world, spiritual empowerment) and what has not yet appeared (new heavens and new earth, the visible rule of Christ, the end of death and radical evil). If a movement confuses those two categories and gets unrealistic about what to expect now (regime change, new economic order, the end of death, perfectionism), then it may increase its conflict levels with disgruntled members who don't see results and with alarmed outsiders suspicious of revolution.

But realism about goals is not the only key to conflict resolution. Second, a movement must be realistic about the "enemy." They must be able to predict both the severity of the opposition as well as "the outcomes of conflict situations."[6] If they think a march on Beijing will turn the tide but end up facing a Red Army with live ammunition and itchy trigger fingers, they may be out of business sooner than later. If on the other hand they think the time is right to negotiate some breathing room and do so successfully, they may kick open the door to the power stage and see the movement realize its full potential.

That's not all that Wallace had to say about conflict and the power stage of a revival. Movements that are successful in resolving conflict are described as being "canny about conflict." They accurately gauge the likely consequences of their own moves and of their "opponent's moves in a power struggle." Failure to have this "realism" and intuition about outcomes increases the "probability of failure." In almost every case where "conflict-realism is high and resistance is low, the movement is bound to achieve the phase of routinization," Wallace-speak for changing their world and becoming part of the new landscape. [7]

---

[6]Anthony Wallace, *Revitalization and Mazeways: Essays on Culture Change*, ed. Robert S. Grumet (Lincoln: University of Nebraska, 2003), 1:27.

[7]Ibid., pp. 28-29. Wallace's own summary of his model is worth quoting in full: "Revitalization

What strategies do "canny" global revivals employ to navigate the storm of opposition? Wallace concludes that successful movements will: (1) employ a variety of strategies including doctrinal modification in order to increase the cultural "fit" of the movement (e.g., write a doctrinal statement to dispel criticism of being a cult); (2) modify the vision of cultural change in an attempt to be more realistic (e.g., write an appeal letter to persuade the government that they are not militant or revolutionaries); and (3) accurately predict the consequences of its attempt at conflict resolution with the prevailing powers of opposition (e.g., press the right buttons to get the government off their back).

One more word from the anthropologists. Most students of revival or revitalization movements agree that such movements often care little about political power and focus instead on altering social position. Groups that feel oppressed or negated by a dominant power may seek to alter their depressed social position not by removing, for example, the colonialist government or left-wing dictatorship, but by creating an "alternative culture" that restores dignity and provides a new arena of freedom of thought and action. In a colonial or postcolonial situation, conditions within which revivals thrive, "changing their world" often means a new sense of identity in Christ and an altered sense of group identity in which a collective ceases to feel subordinate to the dominant power (e.g., if Christ is Lord then our fellowship, however insignificant in the eyes of the world, has vast supernatural resources and powers on our side). New status, new structures (more house churches, for example) and new systems (religious freedom, new civil rights, freedom of

movements are defined as deliberate, conscious, organized efforts by members of a society to create a more satisfying culture. The revitalization movement as a general type of event occurs under two conditions: high stress for individual members of the society, and disillusionment with a distorted cultural gestalt. The movement follows a series of functional stages: mazeway reformulation, communication, organization, adaptation, cultural transformation, and routinization. . . . The movement is usually conceived in a prophet's revelatory visions, which provide for him a satisfying relationship to the supernatural and outline a new way of life under divine sanction. Followers achieve similar satisfaction of dependency needs in the charismatic relationship. It is suggested that the historical origin of a great proportion of religious phenomena has been in revitalization movements" (p. 28).

speech, etc.) may be the realistic goals of a typical global revival.

One of the most powerful tools that a revival movement facing resistance can use both to rally the troops and leap frog the opposition is enlarging their story. If the government imposes a "cult" story upon a Chinese house church, by virtue of that narrative they should be harried and hounded. But what if they can change the story? What if their story as Chinese unregistered Christians is connected to the great story of Christianity down through the ages? Andrew Walls has spoken about the double-sided nature of the process of indigenizing the gospel by non-Western groups.[8] On the one hand, a group sees the gospel in terms of the "deep structures" of their own culture. On the other, a group may also connect their local story to the story of Israel and the first-century Jesus movement. Under the influence of movements of Christian conversion and revivals, new non-Western Christians are linked "with the history of a people quite different from their own" which "gives them a point of reference outside themselves and their society."[9] Using this new enlarged story, revival movements acquire new leverage in renegotiating their relationship with their culture, the state or other churches and religions. By seeing their story as the story of the universal church in both biblical history and beyond, house churches transform their sense of identity and in so doing increase their confidence, faith and hope for future success.[10]

The house church movement in China reflects many of the above dynamics in their journey through the power stage. They have renounced any attempt to "seize power." Instead they sought to "alter social position," enlarging their story with a doctrinal statement that connects them to the early church. They are also healing division within

---

[8]Andrew F. Walls, *The Missionary Movement in Christian History: Studies in the Transmission of Faith* (Maryknoll, N.Y.: Orbis, 1996), p. 54.

[9]Ibid., pp. 23-24.

[10]Walls warns about the manipulation of the pilgrim principle whereby groups may capitulate to the dominate power, often of the state, and use the resources of the Christian story to "legitimate some group's economic and social interests." Walls identifies this as "the ever present peril" of "civil religion" (ibid.).

the movement by removing secondary and divisive doctrines from center stage and refocusing the movement on the core revival paradigm of personal liberation through Christ, eschatological vision, mission to the world and life in the Holy Spirit working through the structures of radical Christian community. So much for my guess as to what is going on. Let's plunge into the story and test my hunch.

CHINESE REVIVALISM AND THE CONTEXT OF CONFLICT

Before analyzing the three documents and evaluating how the house churches are handling conflict resolution in the power stage of their revival, some background on the house church revival in China and the opposition it has inspired may be useful. Daniel Bays has argued that the current resurgence of Christianity since the 1980s needs to be seen as part of a revival tradition in which the "seeds for this continuity were sown in the first third of the twentieth century." Revival has become an indigenous feature as well as an indigenizing forced within Chinese Christianity.[11]

The conditions of twentieth-century revival in China were created by the Boxer Rebellion of 1900. The rebellion can be seen as a nativistic revitalization movement that had as its purpose, like all nativistic movements, the removal of foreign influence, especially Western Christianity, from Chinese life. Its failure meant that China experienced in the decades immediately following the uprising a larger Western and Christian presence than previously. As Bays points out "a much larger Christian community after 1900 . . . was one of the conditions that made revivalism possible."[12]

The influence of the Welsh revival of 1904 was important as part of the "internationalization of revivalist expectations." When Jonathan

---

[11]Daniel Bays, "Christian Revival in China, 1900-1937," in *Modern Christian Revivals*, ed. Edith Blumhofer and Randall H. Balmer (Urbana: University of Illinois Press, 1993), p. 175.
[12]Ibid., p. 162. Cf. Richard Fox Young, "East Asia," in *The Cambridge History of Christianity: World Christianities c. 1914-2000*, ed. Hugh McLeod (Cambridge: Cambridge University Press, 2006), 9:456-57.

184

Goforth found himself at the center of a revival in Manchuria in 1908 similar to what had happened in both Korea in the previous year as well as Wales and Los Angeles, it attracted widespread interest. As in the Korean revival public confession of sin and emotional simultaneous prayer characterized the Manchurian renewal. The public confessions of sin in prayer were so emotional that masses of Chinese hearers fell on their faces and together joined in the chorus of weeping. Many reported visions and ecstatic experiences. The global revival had come to China. One missionary was relieved that they would now "cast our longing eyes on Wales no more."[13]

The importance of missionary Christianity should not be exaggerated, however, particularly in light of its abrupt end in 1949. Young describes the "false hope" of Western Christian observers like K. S. Latourette that China would be "saved" by the proliferation of Christianizing institutions such as the YMCA and the growing network of missionary initiated and dominated Christian schools, universities and hospitals. After 1949 "Euro-American" Christianity which in many ways brought about the social ferment that led to communism was a victim of its own partial success. In the words of John Fairbank, the missionary project could not be brought "to a finish" because of the "great revolution" of 1949 which in turn "finished" missionary Christianity.

While it is possible to tell the story of early twentieth-century Christianity as a missionary narrative, the enduring theme of Christian history in China in the last hundred years is the emergence of the indigenous church through these local revivals.[14] In 1910 a Chinese revivalist, Ding Limei, gained national prominence for initiating a student renewal movement in Shantung. He soon became the traveling secretary of the Chinese Student Volunteer Movement. He became known as the "Moody of China." Though his revivals were less emo-

---

[13]Bays, "Christian Revival in China, 1900-1937," p. 162.
[14]The focus on the collapse of missionary Christianity in 1949 fails to give due consideration to the potency of Chinese indigenous Christianity. From the 1980s onward, Young notes, "an out-of-sight Chinese-initiated, Christianity has come to light, which remained alive throughout the chaotic years of the early communist era" (Young, "East Asia," pp. 456-57).

tional than those under Jonathan Goforth in 1910, in some ways they were more significant. The period between 1911 with the end of Imperial China and 1920 was one of those brief moments in modern Chinese history, like the aftermath of the Cultural Revolution at the end of the century, in which Christianity appealed to Chinese intellectuals. Ding raised up a new generation of talented young Chinese leaders who moved into full-time church ministry under the influence of the student revivals. Though independent Chinese churches had existed since 1906, they proliferated in the 1920s.

A new federation of such churches emerged, the China Jesus Independence Church with over one-thousand member denominations. Independent Chinese Pentecostalism emerged by 1919 that was antimissionary and ardently revivalistic. The True Jesus Church swept through Henan and Hunan provinces in the 1920s declaring itself to be the only true church. Revivalism of both national and missionary varieties continued during the 1920s but on a much smaller scale than in the previous decade.

One of the most successful revivalists in the late 1920s was Wang Mingdao (1900-1991). He traveled extensively using his Beijing church as a home base and published a Christian periodical promoting revival in China. A moderate charismatic, Mingdao encouraged new believers to form their own independent fellowships thus planting the seeds of the house church movement.[15] Yet even in this halcyon period, rival visions of revival produced tensions. The missionary-national tension was serious. National leaders often felt marginalized by the powerful missionary establishment. Theological differences also arose. Ding represented a stream of revival that saw it as a revitalization of culture. Bays describes this version of revival as "Christianity as personal salvation and service to nation and mankind." Sherwood Eddy and John R. Mott influenced Ding Limei and his student followers. Conversion was to be followed by public service and cultural change. An alternative

---

[15]Bays, "Christian Revival in China, 1900-1937," p. 171.

version, represented by Jonathan Goforth, was to emphasis revival as "personal experience of repentance" leading to "lifelong occasional renewal and rededication." These lines of tension would divide in the 1920 in both China and America into "fundamentalists" who insisted on "revivalism" and "modernists" who had little use for it.[16]

After the May Fourth protests of 1919, Christianity was seen as a dangerous Western ideology and a very different intellectual climate ensued.[17] Christian revivalism in China persisted, however. Song Shangjie (John Sung, 1901-1944) and Ji Zhiwen (Andrew Gih) began the Bethel Worldwide Evangelistic Band in 1931 using the Bethel Mission of Shanghai as their home base. By 1935 they had traveled more than fifty thousand miles and had conducted some twenty-four hundred revival meetings. Sung was the more controversial of the pair with his practice of "rude" revivalism. Sung denounced liberal pastors, even calling for a boycott of Sherwood Eddy's meetings. Despite his polarizing ministry, he was called by Bays "the single most powerful figure in Chinese revivalism in the mid-1930s."[18] Occurring just prior to the Sino-Japanese War of 1937, the Shantung revival was heavily influenced by the Norwegian missionary Marie Monsen. The revival was accompanied with cathartic "slaying in the Spirit," "holy laughter" and miraculous healing. But perhaps more significant was the input of Chinese revivalists who formed the Spiritual Gifts Society. The years of world and civil war (1937-1949) brought an end to this second period of revival and renewal in modern Chinese Christianity.[19]

After 1949, seventeen years of ever increasing government attempts to control religion erupted in the Cultural Revolution of 1966-1976. In 1950 under the leadership of a former YMCA official, Y. T. Wu (1893-

---

[16]Ibid., pp. 167-69.

[17]The May Fourth movement of 1919, protesting the Treaty of Versailles and its unjust treatment of China, produced a new intellectual climate in which "all the prominent symbols of foreign presence and exploitation in China" were "turned into targets for vituperative denunciation." The mass revivals disappeared for a time. The new nationalism in both Guomindang and communist versions condemned Christianity as an adjunct of imperialism (ibid., p. 168).

[18]Ibid., p. 173.

[19]Ibid.

1979) two new expressions of Chinese Christianity arose, the Three Self Patriotic Movement and the China Christian Council (CCC). These related agencies had similar purposes: the "deforeignization" of Chinese Christianity and the aligning of all churches behind the government and its programs. Government support for the TSPM evaporated during the last ten years of Mao Zedong's rule.[20] By the time of the Cultural Revolution both registered and unregistered churches were swept away.[21]

After Deng Xiaoping's ascension to power in 1977 Christianity enjoyed a new freedom of expression. A new democracy movement flourished, its slogans emblazoned on Beijing's Democracy Wall. Just as startling was the new freedom to talk about religion. In 1978 a conference on comparative religion was held in Yunnan province "with papers

---

[20]Young, "East Asia," pp. 460-61. The full extent of the terror of the Cultural Revolution is unknown. R. J. Rummel's numbers give us some sense of the scope of the bloodshed in China during those years. Rummel has coined the term *democide* for a government killing its own citizens. He estimates that the total number of democides for the twentieth century is 168 million. The Soviet Union was the most violent government of the century with over 60 million government sponsored deaths. Communist China is next with 35 million. Almost 2 million of those deaths occurred during the Cultural Revolution. These are not all Christian martyrs although many are included in the systematic elimination of "counter-revolutionaries" (R. J. Rummel, *Death by Government* [Brunswick, N.J.: Transaction Press/Rutgers University Press, 1994], p. xx). During the eleven-year Cultural Revolution between 1966 and 1976 all the churches of China were closed. The Red Guard "terrorized, purged and killed many Christians" whether from the independent churches or the TSPM. One Maoist radical claimed that "there is no more religion in China" (Philip Yuen-Sang Leung, "Conversion, Commitment and Culture" Christian Experience in China, 1949-99," in *Christianity Reborn: The Global Expansion of Evangelicalism in the Twentieth Centure,* ed. Donald M. Lewis [Grand Rapids: Eerdmans, 2004], p. 98).

[21]Bob Whyte, *Unfinished Encounter: China and Christianity* (Harrisburg, Penn.: Morehouse, 1990), p. 288. The Cultural Revolution was a war against tradition of all kinds. It was a campaign against the "four olds" (old habits, customs, culture and thinking). Though the Cultural Revolution was also a power struggle within the CCP on at least one point all factions of the party agreed—religion had to be eradicated. Fan Wanlan, historian and member of the central committee, reflected the alarm that many party officials felt about religion: "Religion . . . will not disappear of its own accord. . . . [It] will rely on the force of custom to prolong its feeble existence and even plot to make a comeback. When a dying cobra bites a man, it can still wound or kill him. Therefore no matter how little of religion's vestigial poison remains, it is necessary to carry on a rigorous struggle against it on all fronts and to pull up and destroy all of its poisonous roots." (Whyte, *Unfinished Encounter,* p. 288.)

delivered on Buddhism, Daoism, Islam and Christianity."[22]

The reconstitution of the TSPM came immediately. Bishop Wu had been purged during the Cultural Revolution of 1966 to 1976 and K. H. Ting assumed leadership of the TSPM in 1977. Ting's leadership has been controversial. He has attempted with great success in the 1980s to improve the image of the Chinese government in the eyes of the West regarding issues of religious freedom all the while intensifying the campaign against the house church movement at home.

One of Ting's longest standing opponents was Wang Mingdao, a pioneer figure of indigenous Protestant Christianity in modern China. Wang had been openly anti-Western during the republican era and remained so during the 1950s but refused to bring his church under the TSPM umbrella. Imprisoned in 1956 he quickly recanted only to reject his recantation. Re-imprisoned in 1957 (and released in 1979), Wang quietly encouraged the resurgence of an unofficial Protestantism throughout China after his release until his death in 1991.[23]

Lazarus like, the churches of China, both official and unofficial seemed to rise from the dead after the end of the Cultural Revolution.[24] What accounts for this incredible comeback?[25] Philip Lueng identifies

---

[22]Jonathan D. Spence, *The Search for Modern China* (New York: Norton, 1990), pp. 660-61.

[23]Young, "East Asia," p. 460. A fuller portrait of Wang Mingdao and his influence is given in Aikman, *Jesus in Beijing*, pp. 49-50.

[24]Leung, "Conversion, Commitment and Culture," pp. 102-3. Bob Whyte describes the huge response elicited by Pan Xiao's revealing letter in the *China Youth News* in 1980. Thirty thousand people wrote to the periodical moved by Xiao's confession. "I am now twenty-three years old. It should be said that I have just begun to experience life. Yet for me life has lost all its mystery and attraction. I have come almost to the end. I have traveled the path from hope to disappointment and despair. What began with selflessness now ends with egoism." Pan Xiao's despair is socialist despair—a personal admission that the thirty-year attempt by socialism to create the "new man" who exists for others had not taken root in her own heart despite her longing to escape "egoism" (Whyte, *Unfinished Encounter*, pp. 331-32).

[25]Whyte's angle is that Christianity in China before 1949 for all its size and vitality remained too tied to Western expressions. After 1949 and the experience of Marxist liberation, Chinese Christianity has been reshaped into something more indigenous, contextual and inculturated. He implies that house church Christianity (which he questionably calls "home meetings") is marginal both numerically and theologically to this contextual project and is therefore a minor aspect of the story. He acknowledges the injustice of the Marxist view and treatment of religion in China but also sees it as a "judgment on [the Church's] long term associations with Western power and its captivity within the thought forms of the Western world" (Whyte,

six causes of "Christianity Fever" in post-Mao China. Two main categories of attraction can be mentioned. The first is the intellectual attraction of Christianity. Viewed as a set of transcendent ideas that gave the West its vitality during its greatest age of cultural and economic expansion, Christianity is studied as a philosophy of development among Chinese intellectuals who have lost their fascination for Marxism and Maoism. On a more fundamental level, Christianity appeals to the spiritual vacuum in the Chinese heart. Citing a 1994 survey by the Chinese Academy of Social Sciences, Christianity appeals to urban Chinese due to its emphasis on "salvation, hope, redemption, judgment, love, and conviction."[26]

How many Chinese house church Christians are we talking about? No one seems to agree on the numbers. The most conservative are under ten million. Insiders like Philip Lueng estimate the total number of Chinese Christians has grown from around one million in 1949 to approximately twenty million in the late 1990s, double the official estimate but well below house church claims of eighty or ninety million. Even if Leung's conservative estimates are accepted, Christianity is growing several times faster than the birth rate.[27] Given such growth a new collision with the government was inevitable.[28]

Unfinished Encounter, p. 21).

[26]Leung, "Conversion, Commitment and Culture," pp. 102-3.

[27]Ibid., p. 101. Though admitting that the relationship between economic liberalization and house church proliferation since the 1980s is still unclear, Young accepts the estimates of house church Christianity as exceeding "the TSPM/CCC by several magnitudes." He does caution that "all estimates remain unverifiable" (Young, "East Asia," p. 461). Chinese Catholicism continues to be divided between the pro-government Chinese Patriotic Association (CPA) and the independent and pro-Vatican Catholic churches. By Vatican estimates the majority of China's 12 million Catholics are independent of the CPA (ibid., p. 462).

[28]Donald MacInnes documents attempts by the CCP to determine the persistent and resurgent appeal of religion in rural areas. Two government sociologists, He Junying and Liu Shuxian, conducted a field study of Christian women in Lai'an county, Anhui province. From 77 Christians in 1976 at the end of the Cultural Revolution, the number of Christian women had grown over tenfold to 989 by 1983. While the majority of these women were over thirty-five, there were a significant minority under thirty-five who had become Christians. What was the appeal? Personal transformation was one of the most common reasons. Angry and bitter women found a new hope and release through Christianity that transformed their temperament. One woman stated that "if you become a Christian and join our church and sing songs

REVIVAL AND CONFLICT IN THE DOCUMENTS OF 1998

What was Zhang Rongliang's strategy? How effective would it be in changing government attitudes and actions? One thing that can be said is that Zhang and his colleagues have chosen a time-honored approach for moving back into the mainstream. The documents produced by the house church coalition in late 1998 illustrate their attempt to achieve successful resolution using classic Christian doctrine and apologetics. As stated above revivals seeking to change social perception in order to enlarge their impact often (1) engage in doctrinal modification in order to reduce tension with the dominant culture; (2) clarify the kinds of cultural change their movement seeks to achieve; and (3) develop a realistic sense of the likely outcome of the confrontation with the forces of opposition.

We begin with doctrine and the attempt to avoid the charge of "cult."[29] The October "Confession" offers a definition of what constitutes international mainstream Christianity. The doctrinal guidelines exclude those who teach that "Christ has already come in the person of Ms. Deng" [Oriental Lightning]; those who do not accept "all 66 books" of the Bible; those who do not accept the equality of the three persons in the Trinity;" and those groups that teach that church leaders have absolute authority under God "over his smaller servants." The

---

of praise it will solve your depression." The researchers recorded that many of the women who underwent conversion have become more productive workers. They conclude their report by noting that socialism lacks a satisfying spiritual component because "improving material life does not necessarily mean that spiritual life is enriched." Cf. Donald MacInnes, ed., *Religion in China Today: Policy and Practice* (Maryknoll, N.Y.: Orbis, 1989), p. 348.

[29]"United Appeal," p. 5, in Aikman, *Jesus in Beijing*, p. 294. One feature of the Chinese house church movement, given its acephalous nature, has been widespread doctrinal diversity. A number of heterodox groups have emerged. The "United Appeal" claims to represent "Presbyterians . . . the Charismatic Church, the Local Church . . . the Way of Life Church (also called the Full Gospel Church), the Little Flock Church, the Pentecostal Church, Lutherans who do not attend the Three Self churches, and the Baptist Church." They dispute the political misuse by the government of the concept of "cult." The document implies that both the TSPM and the Religious Affairs Bureau has used this designation to imprison unofficial church leaders. In contrast to this politicized use of the term, the "United Appeal" calls on the government to define cult "according to internationally recognized standards" rather than in terms of joining the TSPM.

document goes on to offer fairly standard restatements of seven key doctrines (Bible, Trinity, Christ, Salvation, Holy Spirit, Church and Last Things) with more elaboration on errors in some of the extremist groups. While strongly affirming the triumph of Christ and his church at the end of history, the statement rejects "the church taking part in any activities that seek to destroy the unity of the people or the unification of the Chinese state."

A second feature of the apologetic strategy of 1998 is the revision of goals for cultural change. In the "United Appeal" the purpose of the house churches is to be a channel of blessing for communist China. The cultural goals of the house church movement are wrapped up in this vision of being a "channel of blessing." While in the early decades of the twentieth century, revival movements may have minimized the social and cultural blessing of the gospel, the house church leaders of 1998 are keen to revise the picture. What kind of blessings are envisioned?

"Attitude" makes the claim that "wherever there are more believers there is also greater social stability, higher spiritual civilization, better social atmosphere, and enjoying greater blessings from God." The leaders then express their desire for God to grant China "peace" and to provide the stated blessings "abundantly." As general as these blessing may sound, they are addressing very concrete issues of concern to the new China. With Deng Xiaoping's assumption of power in 1977 a new pragmatism replaced the old ideological rigidity. "Seek Truth from Facts" was Deng's popular slogan. To the four modernizations of agriculture, industry, science/technology and defense Deng added a fifth modernization "in the realm of the spirit" and openly called for the creation of a "secular spiritual civilization." It seemed a new cultural shift had taken place in the aftermath of the Cultural Revolution, one that Christian thinkers might exploit to promote the faith.[30]

---

[30]G. Thompson Brown, *Christianity in the People's Republic of China* (Atlanta: John Knox Press, 1983), pp. 183-85. The third document of 1998, "Attitude" seeks to redefine patriotism along Christian lines. It begins with the statement that "we love the Lord, the Chinese people, and the state." It goes on to declare that "it supports the constitution of the People's Republic of China and the leaders and the government of the people that God established." It reaffirms

This is precisely what the house church leaders seem to be attempting. Given their growing size and influence on the grassroots level, the house church leaders are claiming to occupy a key place in the creating "fifth modernization" that the Chinese Communist Party (CCP) leadership has called for. While official attitudes may change slowly, the carefully worded claim that house church Christianity could be a major force for "higher spiritual civilization" could play well with both cultural elites within China and Christian elites elsewhere.

How realistic is this open challenge to state authority? The strong tone of these criticisms make it likely that the documents intended audience is less TSPM and CCP leadership and more likely intellectual elites in China and the West. The call for a "spiritual democracy" is one with strong appeal for both sets of elites. When the house church leaders express frustration that the government will not allow them to "have communication with churches overseas," this is not only a clear exaggeration but is a strong offensive in the public relations battle between TSPM and house churches for the support of China's international trading partners.[31]

A final matter is the assumed outcomes of the conflict between house church and communist state. As previously mentioned, there is little in this document to suggest that the house churches actually believe that the government will immediately reverse its policy of in-

---

that though the government has persecuted the movement "we do not show a reactionary attitude, nor have we taken any reactionary action . . . we have never betrayed the interest of the Chinese people."

[31]The documents of 1998 reflect a sensitivity to TSP propaganda that the house church movements are simply to dismissed as marginalized fundamentalists. Bob Whyte's otherwise fine study of Christianity in China is marred by his stereotyping of house churches as "churches of the ghetto" who have failed to enlist with the government program of creating a more just society. He criticizes the churches of leaders like Watchman Nee and Wang Mingdao as "exclusivist," "negative," "escapist" and "fundamentalist." Whyte's view of church in society is ultimately one in which some sort of establishment is necessary for the church to influence society. The only alternative in his mind is a "ghetto church" (his term) which due to its "marginal existence on the sidelines of a civilization" is "a denial of the central thrust of Christian outreach." Whyte seems to assume that some sort of Constantinian arrangement of church and state is the norm and that Christian movements that reject this arrangement are deviant and doomed to irrelevance (Whyte, *Unfinished Encounter,* p. 373).

discriminate arrest and imprisonment. The closing section of the third document asks the government to stop persecution, but notes that even if it continues, they will "not complain" but will continue to "love their country and the government, waiting for God to grant them mercy."[32] With such little hope, why expend the effort to change unchangeable minds?

A final phrase in the "Attitude" document may indicate the real intentions of the house church strategy. In the final paragraph of section IV ("Our Attitude Toward Persecution") the leaders profess their conviction, supportable by history, that "although persecuted, the number of believers has increased rapidly—a force that cannot be resisted."[33] While such language may be dismissed as bold posturing it may well be the key to the house church strategy of conflict resolution. If they can so establish their identity to insiders and outsiders as "innocent sufferers" who are attempting to be a channel of blessing in the creation of the fifth modernization of a new spiritual civilization in China, they may well maximize the conditions of further house church diffusion.

It is the future success of that diffusion that provides the greatest hope for radical change on the government's part. Only when the house church movement is perceived as a "force that cannot be resisted" will the state and its religious arm rethink its policies. The creation of this positive perception of house churches from "ghettoized" counterrevolutionaries to an enormous and growing channel of blessing for the country could well assist in the numerical growth of house church Christianity in China until its claims to represent mainstream Christianity in China become difficult to refute.[34]

---

[32]"Attitude" 4.3, in Aikman, *Jesus in Beijing*, p. 306.

[33]Ibid.

[34]The presence of the two invited Western reporters may support this interpretation. A China increasingly focused on economic growth through Western trade is more susceptible to Western pressure for human rights. Within a year after publishing his book on Chinese house churches, David Aikman, now history professor at Patrick Henry College in Virginia, spoke to a congressional subcommittee on religious rights violation in China noting the arrest of Zhang Rongliang and other house church leaders and urging Congress to take action to curb these violations. But the publication of the three documents of 1998 was intended not only

WE HAVE LEFT YOU NOTHING BUT YOUR TEMPLES

Zhang Rongliang, as a key contributor to the documents of August 1998, soon became the acknowledged leader of the unity movement. In 2000 he traveled around the world informing Christian communities of the developments going on in the house churches. By 2004 he was back in jail on trumped up charges of traveling under a false passport. His advanced diabetes became an issue, as family and friends worried about whether he could survive the seven-year sentence. His son, Zhang Jr., reported that his father continued his ministry as an evangelist even in his prison. Murderers and thieves were repenting and coming to Christian faith under his preaching and counsel. Zhang's imprisonment is a reminder that the apologetic strategy of the house church movement has yet to take effect.[35]

Seen through the lens of global revivals, the house churches of China in their three documents of 1998 are getting ready to change their world. They realize that removing the internal obstacle of disunity and the external obstacle of government opposition are necessary to unleash their full power as a missional movement. These documents reject the Marxist master narrative of religion as a poison or opiate, the European master narrative of the church as a department of the state seeking to provide the sacred canopy under which national life is conducted, as well as the American master narrative of capitalism and unfettered individualism.[36]

---

for foreign governments. A larger concern is the worldwide church and the degree to which increased cooperation and support will come from international Christian allies through clarifying doctrinal positions and demonstrating a nonviolent policy vis-à-vis the state. But what benefits might the worldwide church provide? Positive press and advocacy in making the case that such churches are indeed both "a force that cannot be resisted" and "a channel of blessing" that China can ill afford to oppose. A house church movement that is too big to be contained and is willing to become a force of both progress and patriotism is a movement that political pragmatists will eventually seek to accept and exploit.

[35]"China: Zhang Rongliang Serves the Lord in Prison," *Church in Chains,* January 24, 2008 <www.ccfc.ie/node/205>.

[36]On the issue of master narratives in the new Christianity and especially that of American civil religion, see Chandra Mallampalli, "World Christianity and 'Protestant America': Historical Narratives and the Limits of Christian Pluralism," *International Bulletin of Missionary Research* 30, no. 1 (2006): 8-13.

Their new story is an older and more global story. Part of the new narrative apologetic is crafting a new story about a heroic struggle against two dominate powers of a state church and a totalitarian state. As such the house churches are tapping into the traditional narrative resources used by Luke in Acts and Eusebius in his history of the church in the first three centuries. By shaping this master narrative in Christian terms the house churches represented by these documents are changing their status from "ghetto" churches and dangerous "cults" with an "escapist" social agenda to representatives of "historic mainstream Christianity." By arguing that they are productive citizens and allies in nation building, they seek to increase their social appeal and political space thereby optimizing the conditions of their continued growth.

This reflects in some ways the apologetic strategy of the early church. When Tertullian lobbied for government tolerance of Christians he used the numbers argument: "We are but of yesterday, and yet we have filled all the places that belong to you—cities, islands, forts, towns, exchanges; the military camps themselves, tribes, town councils, the palace, the senate, the market-place; we have left you nothing but your temples."[37]

While formal treatises to government officials seemed futile in the second and third centuries, they did accomplish two things. Christianity increased its popular appeal even as it maximized the conditions of growth by ensuring that government opposition was episodic rather than sustained. Similarly, in a China that believes that one should "Seek Truth from Facts," the best argument of the house churches of China may well be numeric.

---

[37]Tertullian *Apology* 37.4.

10

RETHINKING REVIVAL

Lessons from the
Story of World Christianity

He is an African. She is from India or Brazil. He was broken by
colonialism. She was marginalized by tradition. He flirted with despair. She had a dream, a vision, an encounter with the gospel and the
risen Christ in her own language. A light went on. He emerged healed
and whole from his encounter with Jesus and his gospel. She emerged
with a new sense of liberation and identity convinced she was now a
much loved daughter by her Father in heaven. He preached to his age
mates. She promised that the changes in them could become changes
in the people at large, that the personal would become the political. She
watched as thousands came to join the movement. He marveled as men
came around him to help spread the new light. The movement began
locally but could not be locally contained. He aroused the ire of elders,
colonial governments, educators, bishops and good church people. She
called her followers Bakazufu, Abaka, Balokole, those on fire, the saved
ones, and the alive ones.

Her followers saw themselves as the delivered, the born again, the
saints, the brethren and hundreds of other names. Together they
changed their world. They changed their sense of identity, no longer
the oppressed now, but the liberated who formed an alternative society

to the old colonial regimes or the new but sometimes dysfunctional independent elite. They renewed older denominations. They evangelized with remarkable effectiveness. They created schools, churches, clinics, newspapers, books, deliverance services, crusades. They agitated for new laws, new rulers, new deals and new worlds. He brought the world a new kind of Christianity. She was at the heart of a religious revolution that shook the twentieth century and is reshaping the twenty-first. They are the leaders of global revivals; those funny little movements that most Westerners thought had disappeared but which had simply moved their addresses overseas. This book has been an attempt to understand these new kinds of leaders and the local movements they have championed, local movements knit together by the Spirit of God to become a great and global awakening that has created the new World Christianity.

In the story we have told, we have followed women like her through India and China. We have followed men like him through Korea and Africa. We have seen them start movements as diverse as the Dalit revival in Dornakal and the Aladura movement of Nigeria. We followed their revivals as they spread through Uganda, China, Brazil, postwar America and Ghana. We have seen their numbers multiply until the ranks of the revived began to rival almost every other form of Christianity. We can't explain the new global Christianity without them, and yet so far few attempts have been made to come to grips with what these movements are and how they work. This book has been a search for at least some initial answers.

We have asked what these global revivals are. Our answer is that they are *charismatic people movements that seek to change their world by translating Christian truth and transferring power.* (See figure 1 again on p. 201.)

What is this translated Christianity that makes up the content of a Christian revival? We have seen in Asia, Africa, Latin America and the North Atlantic world that personal liberation through an evangelical conversion is an ever-present element in a Christian revival. Whether it is Paulo Borges Jr. in Brazil or Joseph Babalola in Nigeria, both leaders and followers must cross a threshold that brings them into a new land and opens up a path of hope and change. Such a conversion opens the revival participant's eyes to a larger hope. They see history moving toward its culmination in the triumphant return of Christ, and see his living presence now and the display of his powers in healing and miracle as signs of this future triumph. Those who have crossed the threshold from the world into the kingdom of God through Christ bind themselves together through baptism and communion to carry out the mission of God in this world.

Through the use of their spiritual gifts and through radical love to one another that crosses ethnic and class lines, a radical community is formed that is sent into the world to heal the nations. Evangelical activism, whether it is the ending of slavery in the British Empire, the expansion into unreached areas or the decolonizing of the African mind, changes the world and moves history forward. But these positive spiritual dynamics are often compromised by negative ones. New light extremism, old light reaction, conflict between generations or attacks from spiritual forces of deception and delusion can conspire to subvert a new movement and render it impotent. The large majority of local revivals suffer this fate. This book has paid attention to global revivals that sailed safely through these troubled seas and arrived at a new place of change and growth.

We have also wondered how revivals unfold. Our answer is that historically, global revivals play out in multiple stages. They tend to begin with a problem stage in which great volatility shakes confidence in the old ways and traditional institutions of religion and society. Out of this volatility come first old voices that call for a return to the traditions. But more radical new voices emerge, often from the marginalized ranks of youth and women. These new light prophets speak of their own desperate failures under the old paradigm and the emptiness of traditions and old paths to address their situation. They speak of receiving a new light from the Spirit of God, making vivid and alive aspects of the classic forms of Christianity found in the New Testament, often the

Gospels, Acts or Romans. They testify that this new light healed them from their brokenness and hold out the promise of widespread healing for the entire culture.

Out of this paradigm stage comes the power stage in which the new movement collides with both traditionalists and even more radical vitalists that seek to make a complete break with the past, including biblical ideals. If the new movement successfully negotiates these conflicts their movement begins to change the religious, social, cultural and political landscape.

We have sought to look at the movements from the inside out, trying to identify some of the inner dynamics that drive these revivals. I have found a useful answer in the world of missiology. From this perspective a revival is a nexus of three internal fires. The first is indigenization, a powerful push to transfer leadership of the church or mission from either old or foreign leaders to a new generation or to the marginalized. This indigenization was described well in the nineteenth century by Henry Venn when he called for the "euthanasia" of mission after establishing self-governing, self-propagating and self-supporting churches.

The second inner fire is that of inculturation. The rediscovered paradigm of the New Testament Jesus story plunges deep into the worldview and deep structures of the collective consciousness of a group. The message goes to the core where it clashes with traditional values and core beliefs. Out of the psychic explosion caused by this deep clash of worldviews, comes a translation of the gospel into new categories usually highlighted by a vision of Jesus Christ's supremacy over traditional powers of this life or the next.

The subsequent liberating power of this new vision of the relevance and supremacy of Christ lights the final fire of a revival movement. Contextualization takes place, wherein the new movement seeks to change their world in one or more of several ways. Change may appear first on the level of status. The downtrodden or colonized or marginalized now see themselves as children of God, sons and daughters of a mighty king. They relativize the globalization that took away their

Global revivals are charismatic people movements that transform their world by translating Christian truth and transferring power.

Spiritual dynamics (Content factor—What makes a revival Christian?)
- Personal liberation—shift from rejected orphans to much-loved children
- Eschatological vision—shift from fatalism to radical hope
- Radical community—shift from alienated victims to charismatic family
- Evangelical activism—shift from survival mode to transforming mission
- Life in the Spirit—"Divine and supernatural light" who produces the four shifts and orchestrates all dynamics
- Negative Spiritual dynamics—new light extremism, old light reaction, spiritual warfare, generational conflict

Cultural dynamics (Local factor—What are the essential elements that make up a local revival?)
- People factor (indigenization): transfer of power to new leadership
- Faith factor (inculturation): translation of Christian truth into worldview
- Justice factor (contextualization): transformation of status, structures or systems

Historical dynamics (Time factor—How do revivals develop over time?)
- Problem stage: volatility that destabilizes systems
- Paradigm stage: new light, new leaders, new movements
- Power stage: conflict and conquest

Global dynamics (International factor—How do global trends influence local revivals?
- Globalization—Winds from the West: Global shrinkage and sameness
- Relativization—Crisis of the local: will we survive the West?
- Localization—The reassertion of the value of the local
- Glocalization—Revival, resurgence and global expansion of the local

Group dynamics (Variety factor—Why are Christian revivals so different in content and character?)
- Lucan variable: reviving the evangelical impulse
- Galatian variable: returning to the old ways
- Corinthian variable: radical break with past
- Group conflict: the fight for supremacy

Figure 1. Dynamics of global revivals

homes and their heritage. They have experienced new visions and seen themselves in a new liberating light. This status change may lead to structural change where new institutions may be created to contain the movement and express its mission. New churches, schools, clinics, seminaries, voluntary societies for mission and or social and political change may grow out this structural phase of contextualization.

The fullest expression of a revival movement comes with systemic change whereby political, economic and social systems are dramatically changed by the ongoing application of gospel values and concepts in the wider society. Few movements get this far but when they do they often become recorded in history as an awakening, a revival movement with important social and political implications.

Global factors create the larger contexts for these local movements and open up the possibility of the movement entering the global highway and influencing diverse cultures around the world. As economic and cultural forces of a dominant West circle the globe, they have a profound, often negative impact on local cultures. The local seems to get steamrolled by the global. American popular culture captures the young while free market forces create a small number of well off and a large number of unemployed. As the local is relativized and has its confidence shaken, the stage is set for young leaders filled with new light to offer a way out of this nightmare. Revivals of various kinds renew the local and produce even glocalization where the a renewed people take their movement to regional and even international levels and counter the forces of globalization by making the cultural traffic two way and not just one way.

What remains to be said about global revivals? I'd like to answer three final questions before concluding this global story. One question has to do with diversity in global revivals. Why do global revivals vary in Christian content so much? Why do they use the Bible so differently? A second question relates to the human and the divine role in revival. Are revivals God's work or ours? Are there things that can be done to promote or perfect a revival? The third and final question is about revivals and the future. Despite the story of a rising World Christianity that we have surveyed in the previous pages, is the world still becoming more secular? Are Europe and its religious decline the future or is it the exception? Are we leaving the age of secularism and entering a new age of faith?

REVIVALS AND DIVERSITY: WHY DO THEY COME IN SUCH DIFFERENT FLAVORS?

I have traveled with you to different parts of the world. I have shown you revivals that took place in different cultures and languages with people of wildly different ethnicity and history. Yet my emphasis has been to show the common spiritual, historical, cultural and global dynamics that can be detected within each of these outwardly different movements.

What I haven't said enough about are the variables that can make Christian revivals differ significantly in content and direction. If revivals are by definition, as I have argued, charismatic people movements that seek to change their world by translating truth and transferring power, then why do movements that drink deeply of the same classic Christianity differ so widely in preaching and practice? What do East African revivalists with their emphasis on "nothing but the blood" have to do with health and wealth churches? What does the revival of American evangelicalism have in common with Dalit movements in India or the Korean Pentecost? For all my emphasis that there is a common pattern in all these revivals, I must also admit that there are significant differences also. Why is this so?

As with so much of the theory proposed in this book, I point the student of revival to an insight from Anthony Wallace. For Wallace revitalization movements (that larger family to which Christian revivals belong to) differ according to how they see and use the past. Nativist movements are backward looking and tend to revere the recent past and current traditions. Such movements tend to be reactionary since they are suspicious of change to begin with. A second variable of revitalization/revival movements is vitalism. Vitalists reject the past as strongly as nativists adore it. They see the past as holding back a bright and beautiful future for their group or for all humanity. Vitalists tend to be revolutionary in that want a clean break with tradition and desire to start things over again the right way.

Wallace identified a middle type between the vitalists and the nativists. These were the revivalists. They wanted a beautiful tomorrow just like the vitalists. They also admired much about tradition like the nativists. What permitted the revivalists to be selective about what they wanted to see changed and what they wanted to see preserved was their commitment to an ideal past, a sacred charter lying at the fountainhead of their civilization or religious tradition. Drinking deeply from the sources of the tradition whether it be the sacred Vedas of the Hindus or the book of Acts for Christians, provided the distinctive power of revivalist movements.

Since we have been looking at revivals all the way through this book, it would seem that Wallace's way of differentiating types of movements has little applicability. Don't all Christian revivals seek to go back to the basic and drink deeply from the original sources? Yes and no. I think if we take a slightly deeper look at our collection of revivals we may see that there is more than one way to read the Bible.

If I were able to interview an Azariah, a Babalola, a Kil Sun Ju or a Billy Graham and ask them what where they got the power and inspiration for the movement with which they were associated, they would each say the Bible and the Spirit of God. Each would claim that their revival went back to the sources of the Christian movement itself.

Deeper inquiry however may show something slightly different. Nativistic elements may well show up in a Youth for Christ revival in the 1950s as well as in an East Africa revival centered in Uganda in the 1940s. Vitalism may appear in some of the neo-Pentecostal movements sweeping over Latin America and Africa. Yet the profound love for the Scriptures and declared dependence on the Spirit of God would point in another direction.

One way to answer this issue of why Christian revivals, however common the dynamics that shape them, differ so greatly at times in theology and Christian practice is to look more closely at the first Christian revival in history—the original Jesus movement.

Jesus was a new light leader (par excellence) who started a people movement outside the official temple religions of his day. The movement sought to change their world by translating Old Testament truth and transferring power from priests to apostles. This movement inspired a number of followers and subgroups. Three subgroups can be identified that fit somewhat loosely into the nativist, vitalist and revivalist types suggested by Wallace. In order to adapt his categories to the realities of Christian movements that all seek to use divine revelation as the source of their renewal let me suggest the categories of Galatian, Corinthian and Lucan types to distinguish global revivals of a Christian variety then and now.

The Lucan variety bears the marks of Luke-Acts, namely a strong focus on the person and work of Jesus Christ as the key to salvation and the key to history. His centrality, uniqueness, deity and full humanity are central. At the same time a Lucan movement recognizes that in his risen and ascended state Jesus now rules his world and his church by the Holy Spirit. Because of his elevated place and power, he is in charge of the mission of God which he empowers us to join. So a Lucan revival is one in which the paradigm proclaimed and the practice of the radical community reflects a focus on the centrality of Christ, his cross, life in his Spirit and in mission to the world.

A Galatian movement is one that affirms much of the Lucan variety but would also have countervailing tendencies. Galatian revivals are often characterized (using Paul's letter as a guide) by so strong an emphasis on religious tradition that they may eventually become enemies of the new movement. Paul suggested that about the Galatians (cf. Gal 1). In many of the revivals surveyed in this book there were early advocates who became later enemies. Anglican leadership in Uganda during the Balokole revival seemed amiable at first but gradually became more hostile to the revival which had attacked institutional leaders and traditions. Galatian revivals emphasize law, custom and religious tradition and tend to be old lights. When the Galatian variable becomes too strong it can threaten to obscure the Lucan elements and the Corinthian elements that are part of a healthy Christian revival.

At the opposite end of the spectrum are Corinthian revivals. They tend to reject the legalism and traditionalism of the Galatian revival. They drink deeply from the Lucan sources. What lingers in their heart, however, is the freedom in the Spirit rather than the historical record of Jesus. Both are there but the former tends to eclipse the latter. The experience of new power, new revelations, new gifts and wonders and signs makes history pale in contrast. Tradition seems dull compared to the experience of direct encounter with the Spirit unmediated by priest or protocol. Corinthian movements (some Aladura, some neo-Pentecostal churches and some Chinese house churches) are an important corrective to Galatian stagnation. At the same time they may eclipse the center, the gospel of Jesus and the Spirit whose main miracle is enlightening hearts and minds to see the centrality of Jesus.

All these variables are present in virtually every global revival but certain elements stamp their particular character onto a movement over time. One of the ways we can act as agents of renewal ourselves (if we have access to a local movement that is part of a global awakening) is to seek a reform in which the secondary elements of a Christian revival (that is, a healthy Galatian respect for religious continuity and a vital Corinthian emphasis on life in the Spirit) are restored to their proper place as servants of the Lucan primary elements and not substitutes or rivals of it.

Why do global Christian revivals differ so much? Because they always have. The values of the human heart, love of the past, longing for the future and the new element of treasuring Jesus as the Lord and Savior who makes us fully alive by his Spirit are ever present in a Christian revival. But they can clash. What makes them differ has to do with which set of values dominates.

REVIVAL AND REFORM: HOW DO YOU BOTTLE LIGHTNING?

Related to the question of the differences between revivals is the question of agency. Are global revivals acts of God or inventions of humans? Can I plan a global revival and pull it off through a combination of careful preparation and talented performers? Or are revivals hands off propositions. Are they so much an act of God, like creation, that to suggest a human role is almost heretical?

A careful reading of the story that we have just told makes it clear that revivals are both divine and human acts. The old theologians used to talk about concursus, an aspect of the doctrine of providence in which God is the primary agent of all that happens but that he chooses secondary causes through which he exercises his sovereign rule and causation. As a believer I affirm the concursus as the way God advances his mission in the world. He produces these theoanthropic (divine-human) events called revivals.

Some earlier historians of global revival (I think most notably of J. Edwin Orr) so emphasized divine causation that there was little role for humans to do besides pray and preach. More sophisticated models, such as Edwards and the update on Edwards provided by Richard Lovelace make clear that there is a place for reform in revival. What this means is that whenever the norms of spiritual health and classic Christianity are corrupted or marginalized at any given time in history, there will often be a call for reform by those who are sensitive to the clash between founding ideals and current realities. Luther in the sixteenth century or Azariah and Paulo Borges Jr. in the twentieth are examples of reformers who called for change even as their movements were creatively translating Christian truth in new ways that would rearrange their worlds.

Both Edwards and Lovelace see a role for reform as a prelude and a postlude to revival. The condition that gives rise to a cry for reform is the phenomenon of dead orthodoxy. As reformers seek the help of God and act to bring reform, the Spirit of God may so bless their efforts that a renaissance takes place, a new birth, in which the renewal of healthy spiritual life and mission is restored after a time of corporate decline.

What are the norms of healthy spiritual life that we should work toward even as we await God's empowering work? Richard Lovelace has come up with a useful list of both primary and secondary elements of spiritual health that authorize both the work of reform and revival. Primary is the renewed sense of divine love and empowerment. Though the three theologies of the Awakening, pietistic Lutheranism, Puritan Calvinism and Wesleyan Arminianism contained many differences, they seemed to agree on the central element of renewal: "the experience of grace in the lives of believers." This experience of grace contained two essential elements that needed to be kept in tension. The first was the "Lutheran doctrine of justification by faith." The second was the "experience of regeneration and progressive sanctification." While some writers have focused on conversion as the critical element in awakening, Edwards would argue that this conversion was one that was focused on Christ and his achievement rather than the self and that this new Christological focus became a way of life leading to ongoing Christlike living and values. These two elements became the heart of the live orthodoxy animating the Awakening.[1]

Jonathan Edwards examined the phenomenon of dead orthodoxy with great insight. Presiding over a large congregation of Puritans on the frontier of American expansion and trade, he puzzled over the lifeless profession of biblical truth on the part of many of his parishioners. His conclusion was that truth alone, even biblical truth, is not enough to change the heart of a person. A true psychological and spiritual transformation in an individual can only be effected by an act of God. This is what Andrews Walls would call the translation principle. Edwards noted that in the 1734 Northampton revival few if any new truths were claimed. Rather old truths came alive. These old truths had been seen in a new way, by a kind of sixth sense which Edwards labeled the "sense of the heart." Lovelace claims that for Edwards live orthodoxy "is only

---

[1]Richard Lovelace, *Dynamics of Spiritual Life* (Downers Grove, Ill.: InterVarsity Press, 1979), p. 43.

found where the Holy Spirit opens the eyes of the heart and imparts a vision of the true God and the actual human condition." Such a sense of the heart "changes the whole direction of life."[2] Edwards thus strikes a strong charismatic note. The normal role of the Spirit in an awakening was not "that of revealing new truth but of illuminating truth already given, making it real in the minds and lives of believers."[3]

I have pointed to the spiritual norms of global revivals as essentially four—personal liberation, eschatological vision, radical community and evangelical activism—all seen in the context of life in the Spirit. Lovelace breaks down these essentials in a different way but they make the same point. Spiritual health is not a mysterious goo. There are identifiable norms that constitute healthy vital churches relevant to God's mission in the world. When those elements are distorted or corrupted, we need to work to change them. We pray, we preach, we protest, we plan meetings, we create new structures, we train new leaders, we write books, we send e-mails. The list of reformist activities is long. At the end of the day every biblical reformer realizes that without God we are nothing. At the same time biblical models of renewal give us warrant for a very strong dialectic between human reform and spiritual revival.

REVIVALS AND THE FUTURE OF OUR WORLD

Our final question has to do with what global revivals have to tell us about the future. Are we entering a new age of faith, analogous to the Middle Ages, as suggested by Philip Jenkins in *The Next Christianity*? Or do global revivals point to the last gasp of non-Western irrationalism, which will eventually be tamed by the processes of globalization and modernization? I would like to suggest that global revivals point neither to the return of theocracies nor the eventual triumph of rationalism and secularism. Instead they point to a world of increasingly radical pluralism. What do I mean?

---

[2]Ibid., p. 277.
[3]Ibid., p. 278.

Jonathan Edwards speculated about the meaning of the Great Awakening for the future of history. He was a postmillennialist, confident that the gospel would conquer all areas of sinful resistance prior to the return of Christ. Edwards conceived of revival not as a highly orchestrated moment of religious agitation but rather as an "outpouring of the Holy Spirit which restores the people of God to normal spiritual life after a period of corporate declension." Periods of decline and awakening alternate in both biblical history and postbiblical history.

Edwards as a postmillennialist believed in four postbiblical stages to human history. The first was the calling of Gentiles in the first century. The second stage was the overthrowing of Roman persecution and the establishment of Christianity under Constantine. A third stage is the "establishment of a revived church in a new state of purity and glory to rule among the nations for a thousand years."[4] The final stage of history will be the return of Christ and the establishment of the kingdom of God on earth. Edwards saw America as playing a central role in this eschatological vision of history. As Lovelace summarizes: "A revived American church would serve as a base for the missionary expansion of the gospel until all the earth was filled with the knowledge of the Lord as the waters cover the sea."[5]

Yet Edwards did not believe that this triumph of the gospel would be progressive but rather serial, marked by the wave action of ebb and flow. Commenting on Edwards' *History of Redemption*, Lovelace notes the serial nature of Christian history. Christian history bears complicated witness to the fact that "God's kingdom is like an expanding circle of light in the world's darkness, alternately drawing inward in periods of decline and pulsing outward in an increasing circumference" during revivals. "Thus spiritual awakenings comprise both punctiliar movements in history in which the Spirit is outpoured and also succeeding periods, often decades long, in which the spiritual advantage so gained is implemented in the destruction of the works of darkness, the

---

[4]Ibid., p. 40.
[5]Ibid., p. 41.

purification of the church and the ingathering of the elect."[6]

Lovelace, following Edwards, also accepts that the spread of the gospel is not progressive but serial. "History may be considered," he writes, "as a series of stages in which one territory is substantially conquered for Christ," only to be followed by a contraction which in turn yields to "a renewed Christian assault" which "sweeps outward to widen the diameter of the reign of Christ."[7] No matter what millennial position a Christian observer may take, this "pulsating series of advance and temporary fallbacks" is "consistent with a theology of history grounded on the assumption that the church will continue to experience massive general awakenings right up to the end of its career in history, when Christ will return to deliver it from the last and greatest counterattack of the powers of darkness."[8]

If global revivals add credence to a view of history in which Christianity makes its way through a series of pulsations, then what kind of world does this produce? Beyond theocracy or secular utopias lies a world of growing religious pluralism.

David Martin has a number of fresh ideas about the nature of secularization. Following Charles Taylor, Martin disputes the idea that secularism has as its main meaning the triumph of unbelief over religious faith. This is a secondary meaning of the term, however. Originally, back in medieval Europe, it meant little more than the reclaiming of more and more areas of human activity from the clutches of the church. That meaning is still relevant but gives way to a larger meaning of the term. For both Taylor and Martin the primary secularization going on around the world is that of pluralization, the breaking up of religious and ideological monopolies and the creation of free space in which both civil society and diverse religious expressions can flourish.

Creating free space is an outcome of the serial nature of Christian movement in history. "I argue," writes Martin in language that echoes

---

[6]Ibid., pp. 68-69.
[7]Ibid., p. 426.
[8]Ibid., p. 427.

Edwards, "that instead of regarding secularization as a once-for-all unilateral process, one might think in terms of successive Christianizations followed or accompanied by recoils."[9] Martin speaks of the Christian dialectic between the world and the kingdom. Christianity advances and changes the world. Christianity's very success turns against it. The new norm becomes secularized as a fallen world uses the reformed and renewed structures, and turns them into "the world," a cultural Babel project in which human self-reliance and self-glory dominates. New generations respond to these "reversions to nature" with dissatisfaction as the structures of society become moribund and offer little more than extra channels in high definition. A new wave of Christianization restores kingdom values and perspectives and revives the Christian paradigm. The dialectic continues, however, with periodic "Christianizations" punctuated by temporary "secularizations."

Martin makes clear however this tango of world vs. kingdom produces a spectacular result: the end of power monopolies. When churches succumb to the temptation to join an established order and share in temporal power, they soon become part of the world and cease to be relevant to the kingdom. What Christian revivals do is shake up the system and pluralize power. They create communities of counter power and religious choice. Martin sums up the impact of the Christian dialectic in history by describing evangelical impact in Latin America:

> What we have initially as a consequence of the Evangelical upsurge is the creation of an autonomous social space within which people may participate in the creation of a different kind of sub-society. In this sub-society, those who count for little or nothing in the wider world find themselves addressed as persons able to display initiative and to be of consequence. . . . Moreover, as these enclaves multiply, religious monopoly breaks down and pluralism develops, mediation gives way to direct access, and a competitive religious economy is established.[10]

---

[9]David Martin, *On Secularization: Towards a Revised General Theory* (Aldershot, U.K.: Ashgate, 2005), p. 3.

[10]David Martin, "The Evangelical Upsurge and Its Political Implications," in *The Deseculariza-*

Revivals, as people movements that change their world, are a crucial part of this Christian dialectic between world and kingdom. Their legacy is not Christendom but pluralism and the increasing of freedom in the religious sphere. The future we face is one not of dominant theocracies clashing with secular democracies. The bigger future is the expansion of religious freedom through the pulsations of global revivals over time.

THE SUM OF THE MATTER

I have come a long way in my journey to understand revivals. From the fundamentalist church of my childhood where Bob Jones Jr. brought "revival" to our town through organized meetings to the wild car rides with Paulo Jr. trying to capture the essence of *Sal de Terre* in Brazil, I have come to see that revivals are worldwide. They are neither American folk rituals nor are they exports of a Western religious right. They are, as we have said so frequently in these pages, charismatic people movements changing their world by translating truth and transferring power. They vary in quality, are responsive to reform and human agency, and will change our world in powerful ways as they subvert ideological and religious monopolies now dominating our world.

Like the San Francisco fire of 1906, the rise of the new World Christianity has been both sudden and explosive. Philip Jenkins was not exaggerating when he said "that it is precisely religious changes that are the most significant, and even the most revolutionary, in the contemporary world."[11]

There were lots of reasons for this religious revolution. Globalization, the modern missions movement, translation of the Scriptures, decolonization and the empowerment of indigenous peoples. What I have argued in this book through case studies and theoretical analysis

tion of the World: Resurgent Religion and World Politics, ed. Peter L. Berger (Grand Rapids: Eerdmans, 1999), p. 41.

[11]Philip Jenkins, *The Next Christendom: The Coming of Global Christianity* (New York: Oxford University Press, 2002), p. 1.

is that for most members of the new World Christianity these forces were experienced through the delivery system of global revivals. In one of the many ironies of a sovereign God, the twentieth century, the most secular century in history, created the conditions for grassroots revival that may well be producing in the twenty-first century new spaces for a global faith. Paul called this power out of weakness. Jonathan Edwards called it a great and general awakening. He further predicted that "it is not unlikely that this work of God's Spirit, that is so extraordinary and wonderful, is the dawning, or at least a prelude, of that glorious work of God, so often foretold in Scripture, which in the progress and issue of it, shall renew the world of mankind." In this vision of revival and its potential, as in so many others way, Edwards was way ahead of his time.[12]

---

[12]*The Works of Jonathan Edwards*, vol. 4: *The Great Awakening*, ed. C. C. Goen (New Haven, Conn.: Yale University Press, 1972), p. 353.

Index